Slow Poetry in America

SLOW POETRY IN AMERICA

Dale Smith

For Sarah —
A Time Machine
April 2014

CUNEIFORM PRESS 2014

ISBN: 978-0-9860040-9-4

Acknowledgments

Portions of 'Inside Seeing,' 'Tihama,' and 'Al-Youm' appeared in *Xcp: Cross-cultural Poetics*, No. 12, edited by Mark Nowak; 'Reading Philip Whalen,' 'Philip Whalen II,' 'Whalen's Self-Portraits,' and 'Self-Portrait Sad' appeared in *Jacket* 5, edited by John Tranter; 'Bomb,' 'Kolkota,' and 'Albatross' were published in *Liminalities: A Journal of Performance Studies* 9.4 (November 2013), edited by Michael LeVan. I thank those supporters of my work along with the readers whose comments helped inform the final presentation of *Slow Poetry in America*: Joshua Beckman, Anselm Berrigan, Stacy Blint, David Peter Clark, Andy Fitch, Morgan Holmes, Mike Luster, Farid Matuk, Hoa Nguyen, Laura Pinney, and Kyle Schlesinger.

Published by:
Cuneiform Press
www.cuneiformpress.com

Distributed by:
Small Press Distribution
1341 Seventh Street
Berkeley, CA 94710-1409
Tel. (800) 869-7553
www.spdbooks.org

One's own origin is both real and imagined.

— Peggy Phelan

Where do we find ourselves?

— Ralph Waldo Emerson

Who am I? What kind of man am I?

— St Augustine

If I listened to the words issuing from my own mouth, then I could say that someone else was speaking out of it.

— Ludwig Wittgenstein

But first, are you experienced?

— Jimi Hendrix

CONTENTS

BOMB

In a dream I am old, walking through a small co-op grocery store before its makeover into an upscale food boutique. I see a young woman pushing a cart with two children. I approach and say their names, anticipating smiles. And then I look again. This is not my family, just an image projected from long ago. I am old, my children grown, my wife old, too. The grocery store erodes under broken glass—the drag of time marks it with decay. The sun whitens the surface of the parking lot.

When I wake up I'm in bed with my family on a spring morning. The children run naked, playing monsters. They dress in shorts and t-shirts to play outside. By the window I see how they pass through patches of shade in sinewy release. Their bodies move between the possum haw and plumbego, arms winding in circles above their heads. The world will end, or it ended, or it won't. There will be loss and acquisition. A narrative of world-endings violates my sense of the every day, the ordinary. We grow old, lose ourselves, discovering new capacities in our lives: the child, the spouse, the parent. What do they mean, those many names? What am I in a sequence of events, rearranged by the ongoing drift of memory and narrative, the daily utterances of experience? Are there politics of self-inquiry where I stand apart to judge myself in myriad arrays of self-location?

My old man future self looks back at me down a long corridor. At the other end, Slow Poetry in America watches me play in a yard near my mother's garden. The phone rings. The children run. A persistent memory shaped and reshaped in the play of the present streams images from far away. The boy loafs under a ligustrum hedge, the afternoon sun bright on green leaves. He's alone, listening for the music of a snow cone truck.

Many times I pretend I'm someone I'm not—a cowboy, a superhero. I run off across the yard into a narrow street, arms reaching forward as if to fly. The location of my neighborhood exerts itself through forms of playful dallying, say, in the hot summer. Like many of my generation, thought races to catch up with enthusiasm; emotional awareness glimpsed in crises unfolding.

Once, Donny Green frightened me when he told me the world would end in a firestorm. Bombs on missiles were aimed at us from Russia. The world was rigged for destruction. The memory remains distant. It's difficult to see Donny's eyes, his blond hair and lanky form. His German mother survived the Second War by marrying a US soldier. Her English came to my ears with extraordinary weight, entering my body with dense shapes that dislodged in me a more familiar exchange of words. I was shy to speak with this jolly woman, her cigarettes releasing thin trails of smoke into the air around me. I glimpsed her belly when she reclined on the sofa in her living room.

Back in the driveway, the sun burned through branches of a plum tree above a chain-link fence. The world could evaporate. The world could dissolve under the heat and pressure of vast bombs. I imagined the falling flames, but could not comprehend the totality of such devastation. By contrast to the Flood, there was no covenant between humankind and God to forestall the world inferno. The boy's fright perhaps played in fantastic apprehensions of what death brings, for it was an individual consumption of information, and nothing more, to carry out his haunting.

Donny's mom's German voice carried across the street.

He said men had hair on their penis.

On their penis, I said, incredulous.

On, he said.

Perhaps he got the preposition wrong because of his German mother's English. I thought he must have meant 'around.'

I hoped Donny was wrong about nuclear bombs and infernos and the end of the world. He ran home, his feet hitting smooth pavement. Sycamore pods lay in the grass and on the concrete drive. I crushed one with my sneakers, stooped to lift it, pulling apart the tiny seedlings, and watched as they sailed off into the wind. I took bark from the tree and crunched the brittle roughness in my hands while waiting to chase the music of the snow cone truck.

My mother carried clothes to the line. I went to her. I asked if bombs would blow up the world.

She said, no. But, I said, there are bombs. Yes, she said, nuclear bombs.

I don't remember what else she said. Or what I

felt or said or did. How do you reconcile certain facts? The impact provided a blinding moment of violence, but the ashy fallout promised an afterlife of pain.

When that boy looks forward through time to me now, I think of nothing to say to him. He goes back to the sycamore by himself. He's not looking for his mother. Not listening for the snow-cone truck. Donny Green's mother's voice fills a street called Slow Poetry in America.

AT ATTENTION

One thing my father said to me so often I began to believe Slow Poetry in America was saying it was this: pay attention.

I would spin stories to myself and mostly enjoyed being left alone. I remember putting my ear to the cool metal pipes of the swing set. It smelled like rusty steel. I remember a wasps' nest tucked away inside a corner of the top of the swing set beside a slide, and I watched the insects buzz around, crawling through papery cells.

Slow Poetry in America said, pay attention. But what does it mean?

I saw wasps and tasted the metal on my hands. Sometimes I would climb a mulberry tree beside the swings and sit on a limb and heed the sun through the leaves. Slow Poetry in America was perched invisibly above me in the smooth mulberry-barky shade.

My father clanked around in the garage. He called my name and Slow Poetry in America eased into the waspy buzzing and into the chlorophyll green of the leaves and became so small I could not hide my shame when it was my father saying it to me: Pay Attention.

SCARF & HOLSTER

We tell stories to ourselves, often alone, suddenly dislocated from habits of self-preoccupation. (Or, really, we are disintegrated into bodies of feeling that we had never recognized, or, perhaps, only forgotten.) As a boy, I turned the wheel of narrative through me, portraying heroic deeds of medieval knights, or performing superhuman feats prefigured in the abundant strengths of Superman or Batman. I recall a double holster and pistols, dark blue denim, a blue scarf that belonged to my grandmother, and cowboy boots. I would portray scenes from TV westerns or navigate the images of a John Wayne that so often lit up the nighttime on my father's television. These dramas occupied me on the swing set in early spring, or as I rode a bicycle in circles on the driveway. I see a boy somewhere now in the far distance of imagination as he cinches with a safety pin a red towel around his neck. He reaches forward with his arms to fly into the yard, or through a house among the now long-forgotten items of a people he no longer knows. What was missing remains important: there was no interpretative action to dismantle his heroic desire. Only the drama figured closely in the drive toward imagined forms of connection that, unbeknown to him, contained viral seeds of contraction and doubt. The appeal of heroic measure is matched so often by the dull stupidity and violence celebrated by its form. There is a war at the origin of Western imagination: rape and plunder sustain the projective discourses of cultural representation, and so fire the telling of the tales of Achilles or Odysseus with an authorship internalized by brute recitation or replay.

It used to be that our stories thrummed with tribal narrative—such yarns made sense of experience, or shaped our connections to others, and to things. But heroic drama also forms attitudes and beliefs that converge in needless tragedy. Narrative is composed in part by our reflexes, in tonalities of voice and the particular instances of our words. The interpretive skills required to gain access to the fuller dimensions of narrative are derived slowly, and too easily dismissed in cultures charged by mass mediation and consumption. I recall those who knew how to tell a story, their voices rich with the textures of life more than with the exuberance of some tremendous episode. It takes little to narrate a tale in terms of the duration of event and experience. Instead, we are required to speak intimately to the other, though with a respect for distance, too. Stories are ours insofar as our experiences generate reflection in others, stunting the passions and reactions that so often extend a suffering that can give narrative its prophetic strength. At least, these are some things I have told myself from time to time, given to narratives—ones I am not sure how to possess—and yet, they take me even as I dismantle them, piece by piece. Perhaps in my submission to the demands of the tale—an illusion that interferes with the linear grade of our progression—I arrive not entirely a whole person in any standard sense; determined, instead, by what Freud called the kettle logic of the dream-work: inherent contradictions, confused pathways, disoriented self-composures. Slow Poetry in America advances sideways and backwards in the mouth of what I remember.

COUNTRY & WESTERN

How did I first discover Slow Poetry in America? Not through Richard Brautigan (I found him much later on a book cover with a statue of Benjamin Franklin in San Francisco). I guess it was country and western music.

Summer 1977.

Tammy Wynette performed with humility and gutsy glissando in the South Garland High School auditorium. I was nine years old and remember the vinyl seats and moody lights as the steel guitar slid into bluesy wailing.

Charley Pride played the much larger Dallas Convention Center that same year. My father took me for Chinese food for the first time, then to the show.

I remember frosted hair and denim suits. I remember the weird tension between rural folk-ways and modern conveniences of dishwashers and air-conditioners. I remember chicken à la king and cans of Campbell's mushroom soup. *The Lone Ranger* television series prompted an imagination for adventure that brought to life the myth of outlaw and outsider as wronged figures of romantic good. There was little to hold onto except the desire to outpace the bad guys, adjust the black mask, befriend the outlaw aboriginal whose consequence existed solely as the wise-but-deferring figure in a drama of collective greed and guilt.

Sometimes an uncomprehending sadness boosted the voices I heard behind heavy bass amps and drums. The Big D Jamboree's earnest honky-tonk bands glittered up from the genetic miasma of East Texas. Those field hands fell into suburban banalities and the manufactured comforts that unsettled narratives anyone might believe. I remember 'Stand By Your Man' and 'Kiss an Angel Good Morning.' I remember the long slide of steel guitars, and something I couldn't name. A country song both recalled an agricultural past while mourning the urban division of emotion and mind. There was no vocabulary to announce the unsettling circumstances of the big city. Faith in the economies of modernity equaled the faiths of rural religions of the South, and so thoughtful self-reflection often only could be uttered vicariously through the affective circumstance of song. In efforts to make the strange familiar, art was reduced to formula, and very quickly the ancient folkways vanished under problems well-known in popular songs: divorce, alcoholism, joblessness, violence.

Slow Poetry in America said to me: I remember how much I loved the beat and voices of manufactured loss (the Product: Nashville) that sounded thin in my father's car radio. Behind those reassuring sounds of anxious pastoral transition were voices that appealed to me because the narrative verses expanded my imagination: only there were no accompanying possibilities to organize thought as a process of self-resistance to the deluge.

CLOSED DOORS

The floorboard of the truck was covered in rough vinyl where I played, scooting from the seat down to the floor and back up, pushing my butt up to the edge and dropping suddenly. I fidgeted on the long drive (before anyone bothered with seatbelts), and pressed my face to the window.

Outside, car lights flashed in the approaching dark, and out on the water of Lake Ray Hubbard, red and green boat lights popped like wet gems in the night. Some fishermen moored near the highway with lights still patiently searching through the darkness for perch or crappie or whatever else thrived as Slow Poetry in America.

I look fondly at the blond head of that child as his face pressed the glass, hurtling over the lake into East Dallas. In 1970, Billboard named Tammy Wynette Best Female Vocalist. Charley Pride won a Grammy in 1971. I remember those voices as the emotional textures of time.

Not long ago, I found Charlie Rich's greatest hits (1972) in a used record shop. His voice stirred nascent longing in my father's Ford. *Hey, Did You Happen to See the Most Beautiful Girl in the World*?

Headlights of the oncoming traffic aimed toward us and vanished. The black expanse of lake pulled away, and orange streetlights illuminated broken glass and shredded tires on the road's edge. A strip of weed and grass separated concrete from metal guardrail and the trash of the fields expanded beyond us to the townlets of Rowlette and Rockdale.

Charlie Rich's voice promised a magic gateway to beauty—some notion of sexuality I couldn't understand as sex but felt as some incomprehensible desire. *And When We Get Behind Closed Doors* arrived to my young body with an urgency of inexperience and half-knowledge, awakening a kind of darkling spirit in me. What was behind those doors? Where did they lead? To the most beautiful girl?

The noise of the highway hummed against my ear when I pressed my cheek to the glass. Beyond the glass, the twilight weightlessness of the bluestem outskirts of Dallas feathered away into a dreamy darkness that blurred out against a featureless horizon of orange haze and occasional spotlights. *No One Knows What Goes On Behind Closed Doors*.

FADE FAR BACK

Slow Poetry in America barters in temporal signs, as though time, or our experience of it, comes in variegated contours, or rooms, through which we meander. I conduct illusions to carry forward a sense of meaningful continuity, though each word is repelled by what's not in sight of it. Swollen shapes migrate through the memory archive. Scary things words hardly describe play with my detonation of what it is I hope to recall and clarify. Clarity—a proposition—impossibility. The resonance of stern materiality shifts to sound and typographic image. The palimpsest fades far back, reaching out after things that mutate through an improvised simultaneity.

MULBERRIES

Two mulberries grew in our backyard. I remember the shade they made, cooling the patio during the long summers. Slow Poetry in America merged with the leaves. At some point, a dream-work between things scattered unconscious folds. I look back at those earliest images of the boy I was but find only a solid materiality in the most repetitive of forms.

Mulberries. Fat, green leaves.
  Balance on a limb. Look at backyard

Fences. Alleyways. Rooftops. See
  up in the greenery and play of light

boundaries indecipherable. Span
  into smooth palms. Taste bitter

bark. The tree's fleshy collop. And so bend
  the stem. Shape into it what you are.

Trade signals with soil and juices. Barriers
  unbound by caterpillar webbings.

Hands on hands. Peculiar contrast.
Skin and the skin of moist leaves.

A MOTTO FOR SLOW POETRY IN AMERICA

One time Slow Poetry in America was smoking in a parking lot in the midday sun next to a truck filled with construction gear. The man wore jean shorts and no shirt; a ponytail hung down his back and his skin was tanned leathery brown.

Hippie, said my mother, and told me to get in the car while she put the groceries into the back of our Buick station wagon.

My brothers and I kicked around in the backseat. I looked out again through the window at Slow Poetry in America. Little scattered islands of grass were swallowed by concrete and asphalt. The man in the jean shorts with the ponytail put out his cigarette. I definitely saw a tattoo on his arm that said: Hang it, Dang it, Shake it. That was the motto of Slow Poetry in America.

THE CARRIER

Words carry through time same as image. I write to cast an illusion formed by the word and image 'I' am the carrier of. To conceptualize experience over time means to address the palpable real haunting with a weight unrealized. Every word or shift of sight spooked by the drift of one's place in the lift of things converges, aims, contradicts in the contrapuntal process of reflection. Figures of imagination address us in patchwork compositions of now. Here I work, the voices of children downstairs filter the room just as outside snow melts from bare winter limbs. And some drift of remote possibility returns. When I speak, the far-off thing delays appearance. I look again, finding nothing but quick glimpses. A child. My childhood. The smell of dirt no illusion of clarity may magnify to the page. Roly-poly doodle bugs curled up in your palm. The far-away spooky time inside comes apart and pretends in itself to cohere.

TOY CART

The jet plane's low hum dully continues behind the clunking of a dump truck, pounding the curb with a tire; a robin hunts worms in the yard while far away birds make sounds that arrive almost as if side by side with distant cars, voices, occasional gusts of wind lifting a tarp or piece of metal to flap mercilessly into the ordinariness of every day; far off a motorcycle engine revs against an outburst of rattle from a nearby window; floorboards creak, my arms leaning on the wooden frame, the sound of the friction of a curtain rubbed between my fingers; I hear steam lift off collard greens, the kitchen bustle filtered through a quiet distance. In the daydream, I follow the waving motion of a lilac by my bedroom window. Blue flowers and bees announce new seasonal warmth, and an avian racket distorts my vacancy: mocking birds laugh through the air at something, flitting in low plum branches. A screen door slams, and a woman's voice carries through the house. The window frames the street, invents its codes, organized like a moving photograph in which busy inhabitants strain for objectivity. The pictures fall apart, and no whole can be constructed: an image coheres by way of brief glimpses, willful attachments. Sometimes the danger of projection interferes, and the illusion sustains possibility until, as a stretched too-thin membrane bursts, all disintegrates to shadow, to a vision of the present, where I write, and words fail to apprehend what there might be one day to know. No matter how hard I look, the image refutes my desire for clarity; it withholds vital connections; it challenges a further division of the interior most points of self; it obscures the objective field of what I hope remains: a form of my possession in memory. The sound of a toy cart pulled over concrete for a moment reenacts the codes of discovery, and the forgetting of one's self.

'68 / '69

It's tempting to consider how the era one is born into preordains certain behaviors or compulsive, sublunary thoughts. Cultural events striate the body with mediated certainties. The television constantly vibrated in my house, reconstructing and dismantling black-and-white narratives that were told to survive what a people constituted as reality. Robert Kennedy's assassination in Los Angeles; the collapse of the Prague Spring; the Yippie 'Festival of Life' at the Democratic National Convention in Chicago; police beatings of marchers again in Chicago in August; the My Lai massacre; the election of Richard Milhouse Nixon as president. Go forward to summer 1969 and consider the Manson murders and Altamont against the dramatic imprint of the moon landing. No doubt the circulation of the news of these events affected me, just as the Great Depression and World War shaped my parents' generation. Still, leaping forward, 9/11 gives social body to the lives of my children. Slow Poetry in America winds through the textual nerves of these temporal locations. A great distance subverts the present with the ongoing shock waves of the past. The narratives thicken stories without meaning. Or their meanings dislodge with such frequency from the textures of reality that prepared them it's hard any longer to accept the violent intensities sustaining them. Time is vanquished into memory and image. To reconvene meaningful substance to one's personal stories requires thoughtful connections of imagination—even as ligaments seem to dissolve, or come untethered, disturbing any metaphoric condition. Slow Poetry in America somewhere pushes the paranoid states of the sixties into a new present. It renders in skeptical fashion arcs of the personal pushing up against impersonal orders of the real.

PACE

Each word arrives new. Speak: the animal presence of the mouth shapes a sonic lift, each sound making a slight impression beyond the tongue and teeth, the warm breath of the body. Back of the throat vibrates with a guttural buzzing. There was much time and to be alone in it brought great pleasure in the do-nothing interior of my imaginings. Where do things go when they leave the body, lost in bending strides of memory and imagination? Share a world in each opening or drift of thought leafing into the seemingly present resources of being here, adrift in place with others.

My mother called my name from the kitchen door, and it carried across the hot patio and into the mulberry shade where I played in a sandbox beneath waxy leaves. The word startled me from attention, and I turned, shifting my body slightly toward her. Come in, she said, I want you to meet someone. Someone: another woman in my house with my mother. I can't say her name now, nor do I apprehend her in memory. In my imagination I see the yellow summer dress my mother might have been wearing. To be called to attention, a word, or name, compelled action. The house was cool, and outside light spread against sheer curtains that played to my eyes. And I said, yes, ma'am, to the woman on our couch beyond the television that was not on. And I listened to her words and my mother's speaking to the other woman, and did not know what to say. My mother gave me a sandwich, and encouraged me to eat as they spoke and I felt words I could not hear; I felt sounds I could not bear: I imagined the shapes of those swift utterances, and took my lunch, with milk, in a kitchen with language inside me.

DEAD RABBIT

Slow Poetry in America lay stiff and dull in its cage. A bare bulb warmed the little plywood and wire cell as the winter wind spread one dark night. The once-wiggly nose froze inert; long ears flattened back against brown fur.

What did I see by the bulb in the cold, my mother's hand on my shoulder?

Slow Poetry in America the Rabbit—aka Thumper.

And I cried because I was a little boy and because there I lived in the bewildering sadness of the continent. My tears were not for the rabbit, but for the cold stony ruins of highway and buildings stolid and soundly displacing the tall plains grasses. Or so I pretend now, as if tears are recalled from memory with any persistent accuracy: the sadness of the boy was confused with attachment, and the object of desire lay frozen in a cage of casual making.

The eyeball of the moon blinked out, and the eyeball of the sun winked awake.

You die, but then you do not die in Christ. The

preacher moderately advised the congregation in his Sunday sermon.

But Slow Poetry in America would not let me believe anything like that. I listened to the hymn. I could hear into the Gospels: that drama came unhinged from any historic specifics. Instead, the stories played on my mind as a force of nature. Something 'spoke' to the 'heart' of the boy in the post-mortem glow of Sunday devotion. The organization of belief, or even attitudes (especially attitudes), toward the personal fact of death, fails to account for experience, the dramatic action a passage creates. But thought itself shapes and restrains faith, requiring stringent terms of inquiry by which to put at ease any hollow nagging impossible to resist. At least these are things I tell myself when looking at the boy on the pew in the Baptist church so far away from me now.

HIDDEN

Slow Poetry in America swirled in the ceiling of my parents' room. Thick, white paint like cream over sheetrock.

The A/C blew cold air, and I felt the smooth satin surface of the floral bedspread. My father was at work, my mother talked on the phone in the kitchen. I heard her voice muffled through the walls and watched the outdoor light play through curtains.

One time I grew upset with my mother over some minor thing. I ran away and felt the summer warmth on my arms and in my hair. I took myself inside and hid between her and my father's bed and the window. I snuggled in close to the floor and wrapped myself in the skirt of the floral bedspread that draped close to the green carpet, listening as she called my name, a name to which I did not respond.

Slow Poetry in America shifted in the light and dust motes of mid-morning sun. Tears dried on my cheeks. A little thing: life's little stupid things are so magnified. When I touched another person's face, or felt the cotton cloth of my mother's dress, knowledge would yield certain specific realities that surpassed my imagination. How I loved the intimate, innocent pleasure of touch.

After a while, my mother panicked and called our neighbors, and soon they were all out looking for me too. The sounds of my name came through different voices, the speech of the mothers on our street as they searched for me. I remained hidden, feeling my power of invisibility over their concern. To break the spell would be to step into the open, to stand against the orders of an otherness that was maternal and instinctively severe. I felt secure in my shroud of bedspread, but grew anxious, and did not know what to do.

Eventually, hearing my mother enter the house, I popped up and said, Here, I am.

Slow Poetry in America moved through me and the curtains and the light and my mother whose disappointment and relief filtered back through the light into the air into the trees and the rooftops and beyond what I could then imagine as love.

SHOOTING

Often, my father put a bottle on a tree stump, or balanced an old beer can. We'd shoot to see who could break the glass or dent the aluminum.

I learned to aim carefully and then to slowly, very lightly, nudge the trigger back until in one smooth action the bullet invisibly shattered the object of my attention.

When I was a boy, about five or six, my father took me to a field in North Texas to hunt dove. He rested the barrel of the shotgun on a cedar post, propped the butt up to my shoulder, and told me to aim and shoot. The force of the gun kicked into my shoulder, driving me to the ground with the dead grass and dirt. I was too shocked to cry at this ritual lesson: it was Slow Poetry in America for real.

In my family lore, spoken in hushed fragments of regret, was the story of Donny, my Aunt Lucy's son, who died during a bird hunt when his shotgun discharged while climbing a barbed wire fence. I never knew him, just his ghost, on the dry tongues of my people. I often wondered about him, the ghostly hunter, my cousin, as I wandered North Texas fields where my family's ranch sustained several generations. Once I saw a calf newly born in November cold, a wet caul sticking to its thin body. The repressed hush of Donny's name occupied the sky and grass. A decayed grain silo focused my attention skyward. Inside I yelled as loudly as I could, throwing my voice up toward an oval portion of sky open as an eye to the blue above.

KOLKATA

My grandfather, Martin Luther, leaned against his El Camino, testing the carburetor. The flat surfaces of the outskirt loam received horizontal pale pressures of sunlight. He played thirties-era jazz: Benny Goodman, Duke Ellington, Cab Calloway. I admired his blue jump suit and Justin boots.

Slow Poetry in America arrived as cold relief, bottled like Coca-Cola, sweet and icy on my throat. Slow Poetry in America, I think of you so often, and how it was then in that great stretch of western banality. Some might call it suburban and bourgeois, but you could see through every instance, every gesture, how each muscle and nerve had grown out of the humid soil and green density of time. Fort Worth, less so than Dallas, adhered above the plains and river basins as a shiny abstraction. It had a zoo and art museums, strip malls, and taverns. Each year a parade led to the city's stockyards in a gesture of fealty toward the past. Cowboys and cattle drives figured large in my imagination, even as I absorbed urban conveniences of air conditioning and automobiles. The past was manufactured to sustain my ease, to put out of reach any special knowledge that might temporarily and self-consciously halt the modernization of the plains. To stop that progress would have meant to fade into insubstantiality as the rest of the nation binged on Texas crude.

In the evening, my grandfather often played his recordings of jazz. He stretched out on a Lay-Z-Boy recliner to read *National Geographic*. Once in a small tin box I found photos he had taken while stationed in India during The War. The years of his service occupied family lore, and even as a child I understood that he had flown planes from what is now Bangladesh over some of the highest mountains in the world. I knew he did not like the test, and that it was dangerous, but he carried cargo over the Himalayas throughout most of The War. More than 4,000 pilots, many smashing into darkness at extraordinary altitudes, were stationed there. But what I recall that day—I must have been seven, perhaps eight—was the discovery of the textures of his experience. Even then I felt that the images I found meant more to me than to him. With a kind of embarrassment, he observed how I was perhaps too young to be looking at such things. He explained how the funerary pyres occupied space on city blocks and that the flames in the photos were of the deceased.

My eyes wandered through the images, in awe of something I could not quite pin down. Human frailty sounds so cliché, and yet here were bodies laid out on the side of streets for final rituals. I think of my own people—the brevity of our lives and the rituals of preservation and burial. A few generations exchange their values and brief possessions even as, in an instant, centuries seem to pass. Who are those people on a street in Kolkata, their trials long absorbed into vast anonymity? I didn't care as a child who they were, actually. I found interesting *what* they were, however, and tried reading into the significance of their figurative placement for me in the tin box my grandfather had brought home from a world far away. Certain textures of experience seize the imagination.

It must have been around this time that Donny Green tested my stamina by announcing the apocalypse of nuclear war. I wonder if I had the capacity then to reflect on what it meant? Certainly, at some level, I understood how life had been seized in advance by regimes of power that included nothing of my experience. I wonder now what possessed my grandfather to take those images from the pitiful figures who gripped the asphalt and dust as the features of their loved ones disappeared from them forever. What were these instances to him and how did they organize meaning in his submission to a foreign culture—or to his own? The sudden and matter-of-fact manifestation of the dead body, perhaps, seized his attention as it claimed mine, years later. I'm quite sure, in fact, that he must have provided money in exchange for the pictures of these dead. I gazed at the corpse of an infant. Because I was at an impressionable age, and because I am also an impressionable person, my grandfather's encounter, however mediated, fused in me with something I still hesitate to name. I see Donny Green under the mulberry trees in our yard. We ride our bikes through the shaded portion of the driveway on a summer day in the nineteen seventies. Locusts scream across the yard. Sycamore branches form a canopy. We race around.

A sense of horror often accompanies moments of ease. Even now, motivated by these black and white pictures, I pursue some knowledge that refuses delivery. I don't possess an easy sense of things. The edges creep in. I see the naked child in the doorway. In the shadows, he appears to be about my mother's age at the time, a toddler. Perhaps my grandfather took this picture because of some homesick sense of relation between the child and his daughter. I wonder about that young pilot still, and his movement from the fields into the air, across an ocean and into a war that compelled him by naïve relation. An organization of character in ratio to vast ideological drives haunts the familial lore—the old force of the Bible and bumpkin pastures replaced with some new but equally forceful drive. I continued for many years to seek out that tin box. When I would visit, I traced through the images to try and see myself through them, and imagine things about the world.

SHAVING RAZOR

Often I'd watch with curiosity as my father shaved each morning. I became so intrigued I asked for a razor, and he soldered a bladeless one for me in his garage workshop. I'd lather my face and press the cold steel to my cheeks.

What this has to do with Slow Poetry in America suggests a kind of primordial encounter. My father's body attracted my attention. I'd run my fingers through the hair on his chest in what now I realize as intimate, casual love.

Once, with my youngest son, I pissed in a public latrine. He looked at me, intrigued, and with complete confidence and pride said, Nice penis, Papa.

The vulnerability of separation from things—from those we love, and the objects we adore as our own—somehow moves us onward into who or what we become. My words form an illusion of order, though back of this I wonder about the cohesions that give shape or form to what we call poetry. And so to arrive into masculine rituals of hygiene, I look with a kind of imagining into possibilities of coerced devotion. Are there choices? Our language—its situated confidence and easy, sinuous presence—perhaps adjusts through bodily intimacies. We receive the material force of words, a fondness for certain pronunciations or usages, almost, it seems, as through touch. The childhood play of babbling sounds filters through the experiment of contact. Over time, the enactment of social boundaries enforces divisions that words often can overcome. Our sounds enter the other. We play there if we can—or witness violent codes that orient familiar borders. In the blink of an eye, my sons internalize limits of social mobility. In the blink of an eye, as if certain features of time collapse, I see my father, my children. A warmth and delight caught by overwhelming distance.

LAKE OF THE PINES

The water's expanse spread for miles as my father powered the fishing boat over the grey surface. My brothers and I would sit on a pier with bamboo rods and fish for perch, mosquitoes biting as my mother arranged the cement-floor cabin. In my memory we are no longer ourselves, but figures of something other. An optimism of my family runs weirdly with elongation, surfacing and dismantling the durable habits of space we are prepared to occupy.

I see myself now as a boy, wearing only shorts. I walk out with my father into Lake of the Pines. The sand oozes between my toes. I hold his hand, the water to my waist. We do not speak, but the sense of movement with him into our separate experience remains strong. We step out hardly there but for the traces of our patterns in damp sand. The water splashes our knees. RVs are parked under pines where life makes curious patterns I no longer recognize in the shade. My mother fries bass, makes hushpuppies. My grandfather's confidence expands from shore, in his lawn chair. These patterns of experience so quickly become other in the memories of my affection. Bolted picnic tables with Lay's potato chips and Jell-O salads await us. The immense power in these figures drifts into the present. Nothing is here but the quiet of a sleeping house at some other moment in time. A cold, dark night in Ontario, far away from that lake and warmth. And yet the years hardly matter. There is no time. And none of us is here, except as specters to memory.

DRESS UP

The performances of gender I witnessed as a boy somehow also admitted the forceful peculiarity of Slow Poetry in America. Texas in the seventies bulged with ideal exaggerations of male possibility. One time I visited my cousins who dressed me as a girl in a skirt and blouse. They did up my hair and put makeup on my face. When my father saw me, his look of disgust went through me with callous intimacy. My face burned with shame as I changed back into blue jeans and t-shirt. I must have been eight or nine. I wondered on the long ride back to Dallas what I had done. In that omission somehow a body of feeling slurred into the pressure of my blood and the sloughing energy of my skin. Part of the experience of art has been for me to understand the hushed, demonic constructions of character from those male silences surrounding my boyhood. A deep shame and urgency to hide feeling, to withhold knowledge I should be proud of and confident in, is denied. But Slow Poetry in America—I trust in it to guide the cruel divisions I imbued even as, in its impermeability, there are contradictions impossible to balance by any means.

DRIVE-IN

I remember being stuck at a train crossing in my parents' station wagon on Saturn Rd next to a drive-in movie theater. Film violence was enlarged above the motor lanes. Perhaps what I saw was *Hell's Angels on Wheels* or *The Wild Angels,* starring Jack Nicholson or Peter Fonda. My mother told me to close my eyes, though I did not. I first saw a naked woman on that screen, as she was groped from behind in an act of impassioned embrace that confused me. I pressed my face to the window and looked at bodies expanding across the screen. The train moved its cargo, the rattling and scraping of steel penetrating the field where cars parked, their occupants poised to watch those moving fantasies.

Beneath white gravel,
the asphalt roadway,
black clay compressed.
Bluegrass blades
held to the soil
meshed with henbit
in chain-link.

Hairy bittercress
and nutsedge,
stuck to things,
unadorned, with
bits of trash
(candy wrappers),
and popcorn.

STRAIGHT FORWARDNESS

In the folds of daily acquisitions and wanderings, or in the quiet, inward decisions of belief and new findings, Slow Poetry in America dwells, a little absence in material abundance. To grasp is to possess, and in that possession a fatal loss adheres like a trap. By adapting to the conditions of the day, the ways and abilities of a culture, everything is risked in transactions that barely hold, if at all. If language can subvert the impulse behind its organization, and if the self submits, a new folly exists in the newly fashioned advantage overtaking the page. In the event I accept my own progress through words, then I leave behind the capability of another, perhaps more qualified, possibility—one without progression, but exchanged in contrapuntal measure, across certain regions of order that carefully dissolve illusions of straight forwardness.

MRS BISHOP

Slow Poetry in America like a rock casually tossed into a creek. Another skips over the surface while the sound of traffic descends the ravine from a nearby overpass. Long, solitary rambles through a dense pattern of leaves and branches and discarded urban debris. The years accumulated and a range of attention spread far out. I remember writing a poem in my eighth-grade English class, and how I surpassed myself despite an outer surface of indifference. I remember turning on to the pattern of words and syllables, and how the energy shifted slightly in arrangement. I remember the sudden buzz of excitement in the making of a book for Mrs Bishop's 'Values' assignment. I remember Mrs Bishop's severe form of care to the sonnets she assigned, and how words framed my desire, releasing and protecting me from the inchoate chance of youth.

PIZZA

Slow Poetry in America dipped snuff and spit in a tin can. Slow Poetry in America taught Jim Beavers and me to play 'Foggy Mountain Breakdown,' 'Billy in the Low Ground,' and 'Black Mountain Rag.' Jim Beavers sang, 'Roll in My Sweet Baby's Arms.' And I backed him on the Yamaha guitar my mother had bought me.

One afternoon when we were twelve or thirteen, Jim and I took his brother's car while he was away at church camp. It was a red Pontiac LeMans. We were in a newish suburb almost within reach of old rural distances and wanted pizza, and so we drove out very cautiously along quiet back roads in the steady heat into town where we ordered a pepperoni.

On the way back home, the car overheated. We parked along the road in a thatch of brown grass under shade of bright hackberry.

Jim Beavers and I wore straw hats and t-shirts. I carried the pizza box, and he strapped a banjo over his shoulders. We played songs taught to us by Slow Poetry in America.

I see those boys in the heat and North Texas fields where houses were abstractly contracted throughout the eighties. I try to look through their eyes years forward to see Jim Beavers become a Nashville songwriter and musician. I weigh the manufacture of product against the optimism of adolescent desire.

TRAMPOLINE

I asked Cathy Schools to go with me in eighth grade. I didn't understand what 'to go with me' meant, but I felt a sexual leap when I said the words. I walked with her after school, along Kingsley Rd and over Duck Creek, to Glenbrook Dr, carrying a trombone in a long, geeky case. I remember a Hallowe'en party and spin the bottle. I remember the incipient stress of desire as I pressed her lips. I was discomfited to see her at school because I would be hard, and I tried to hide it (like anyone's looking—though it felt like everyone *was*).

Ride a bike to Cathy Schools' house.
October cool in the air. Leaves
crunch under tires. Goose pimples
prickle her thighs. She wears a cheerleader
outfit: 'Go Mustangs.'
Her hair is blond, thick. A white
thin strap of bra lace comes
undone under mascot tank top. Look
for words. The dumbest things to say
arrive. To be so embarrassed. The smell

of autumn smoke, like sex. Lean
on the cold steel ring. Her trampoline thick
with leaves of the sycamore.

Mrs Barnes guided the composition with high-lifted eyebrows. The Steinway buzzed as thirty voices reached for the higher notes. My eyes were focused on Tiani Warden, her newly discovered—to me!—figure accentuated by the label Jordache. And then the piano crescendoed my attention: 'I'm gonna live forever / I'm gonna learn how to fly / HIGH // I feel it coming together / People will see me and cry / FAME.'

I liked choir, though I didn't feel that it was making me into much of a man. But then, I didn't want to be shaped as such, though I didn't understand either that alternatives existed. A general awkwardness accompanied every day in my adolescence. I liked being with girls and singing, but it compromised the rigid images of masculinity I thought I was supposed to embrace. To become a man or woman anyway means cutting oneself in half, participating in self-atrophy. In the process, the specter of a fragile inner substance negotiates new potential, and perhaps can, only rarely, overcome the limits of a culturally induced mutilation.

I signed up for the football team and played line-backer. The ball snapped and I thrust myself into the folds and padded boundaries of disorganized flesh. I remember how during kick-off at the season opener the other team returned the ball for a touch-down. It was difficult for me to compete with the required aggression. I'd lunge forward as the ball snapped, reaching for the running back, only to let him slip by me. My disappointment and disinterest developed over the year into what teachers would call a 'bad attitude.' I began to hang out with 'freaks' who grew their hair long, smoked cannabis, and listened to Led Zeppelin.

In the silent hallway after school one day in late autumn, the deserted lockers and classrooms of the public institution seemed cheap with objectified withdrawal. Or was it my own enforced stepping away into the feminized resources available to me that scattered my mind with a kind of awkward insouciance? Whatever the state of my fragile self-invention, Cathy Schools came to me in the empty breezeway and kissed me. I went home and jerked-off for Slow Poetry in America.

NIGHT WALK

One time I crawled out my window late at night to meet some boys I knew. They were older, with shaggy hair, and muscles toned in their arms like the sons of dirt farmers, roughnecks, derrick hands, and roustabouts. I jumped over ligustrum shrubs and ran off to find them.

There wasn't much to do. The oldest boy lit a joint, inhaled the sweet smoke and released. A narrow, urban field spread out adjacent to the Rexall and Piggly Wiggly. A wall made of cement blocks, and in need of repair, separated the shopping center from Caldwell Elementary. Blades of brown grass grew up in the rock and through the stone surface of the wall. Someone tuned into a Dallas hard rock station with a transistor radio as the joint was passed around, and Slow Poetry in America contained us on the grass and rock and urban trash that twisted the geography of my imagination.

I took the joint between my lips and saw stars expanding mightily above the field. I looked across billions of years with the feelings of barely surfaced thoughts. Each blade of grass around me stood erect and glowing in the hypersensitive vacuum of my stoned eyeballs. The field and the sky continued to spread with active intensity, like a history of an entire people compressed by mud; continuously it came to life while other parts winnowed away, dying: the Midwest soil gathered into itself, creature-like, and dispersed.

On the way home down Old Orchard Rd and Caldwell St and Saturn Ave the mulberries and plum trees were spinning. I had a bit of hair on my lip. Peach fuzz, the boys said, teasing me as we walked to Sheridan Dr where I left them to climb again into my room.

I did not know Slow Poetry in America wanted to consume me. I did not know I even had an opportunity to be so called by the voice of the mud being I was a part of, too. Poetry turned out to have been everywhere, and I could see it, but did not know what I saw when I looked out over the trashy escarpments cluttered with malls and apartment complexes. Public pools and parks coagulated a municipal order above cement columns lifting Kingsley Ave over the sludge of Duck Creek; crappy

Duck Creek pulsed limply through abandoned shopping carts; spray-painted genitals sprawled archaically on the slabs and sloping sheets of concrete that had been poured in that slurry decay of brown water.

I lay in bed until the first blue light of day shut my eyelids. And then I slept thirty years, waking to write this and remember Slow Poetry in America only now.

WICHITA FALLS

The wreckage spread out through yards and down streets, homes gutted and exposed, with the collapsed roofs and shattered windows of Slow Poetry in America. Panels of billboards had been blown out and everything possessed a curious patchwork of ruin. It was as if the something prior to disaster had left a presence only by which to punish the memory of place for those whose bodies absorbed the effaced blocks of city waste.

The name of God or Jesus figured also in the city's collapsed form, little crosses and withered Churches of Christ and Pentecostal slabs lay splintered, exposed to the wrath of some greater geography.

In images of the Wichita Falls tornado there are small signs of what's to come, as if some prescience of disaster was withheld by the landscape. The Trade Winds Motel, in one photo, stands against the black force of the tornado. The flatness of the land beyond beckons the wind, those ancient surfaces razed by centuries of invisible weight and the more visible forces of cloud and rain; dense funnel pressures rearrange the scenery, uprooting cottonwoods and mesquites, as closer to the flaked limestone and shale soil bluestem and foxtail bow under atmospheric pressures.

To my mind, absorbed by the feathery cirrus bands approaching from the Texas Panhandle, great freedom and flexibility lay in those giant formations—some pre-human and unspecified force moved parallel to the ongoing dreams and nightmares cut with cement and metal on the plains.

The big sky mirrored geographic terrain, only the atmospheric morphology was composed—and disintegrated—at a more rapid pace. This was a lesson too in the study of Slow Poetry in America, regardless of whether or not I understood it so.

IGNIS FATUUS

Long days of summer unevenly spin.
Past a place of stillness you pass
time in play and labor.
Chinaberry husk. Horizon.
Watch a passage of storms. Black
clouds bloom the internal chimera.
Find a way back to native origin.
Azimuth. No path but what circles
back these days—sound, wording other.

VISITANTS

This is about the Slow Poetry in America vision of lights.

The story begins at a turn-of-the-century cabin exposed and weathered. A chinaberry grew just out the door, its limbs bare, save for a few dried and brittle clumps of yellow pods dangling from its branches. Stock tanks and salt licks and barbed wire stood out on the rocky surface of bristly countryside for miles, a solitary path of limestone veering downhill toward a little ranch-to-market road leading to town.

Cold north wind and exposed limestone glowed on the surface.

Down the stone path toward the ranch's entrance I recall cattle and sheep, clumps of bluestem and prickly pear, as further out the horizon blurred into the twilight.

My father built a fire and we sat, eating hotdogs as the darkness spread. Above us, the Milky Way expanded vast and incomplete. I listened to low voices through a transistor radio.

November's chill drove us inside, and my father put cedar logs into the wood stove and lit a match. Linoleum peeled away in the corners and a layer of grey dust scuffed over the floor. I liked the sulfur of the match, and watched the blackened stick release last trails of smoke. An ancient bureau held pistols and ammunition, grimy oilcloths and metal lubricants.

The alarm woke us at five. We bundled up in flannel shirts and down vests, took our guns and left with a piece of bread or some nuts or fruit. I followed his steps over the rough limestone paths until, veering off, we found ourselves in denser brush.

Nestled deep in the scrub was a deer blind built of oak limbs that had been shaped and entangled roughly. We sat in the cold and waited.

As dawn approached, the life of the countryside began to move. Purple finches darted while further out flycatchers dipped toward a distant horizon, a little stretch of it I glimpsed through the branches of some great oak furzy with mistletoe and ball moss. Squirrels and other rodents made their ways throughout the trees while on the ground were insects—dark beetles—close to my boots.

My father nudged me and, looking up, I saw one, two, perhaps three whitetail deer. Their black noses sniffed the air cautiously. We sat motionless, and I could hear breath move through my body as I tried to imitate my father's stiff pose. He lifted his rifle, sighted the deer, and looked through the scope at their grey-brown bodies. As the morning moved in that dramatic stillness, sunlight spread through the branches. Slowly, the animals turned, wandered off, finally loping beyond view as the last bough of oak or juniper settled on the space they had occupied only moments prior.

We returned to camp with no meat to dress, so spent the day shooting cans. Once, a rattler confronted us: my father aimed. Was there an impact? The coiled form unfurled and slid under the cabin in an instant. Cold, icy wind blew. At dusk we set out again.

One night, after hunting, and after driving into town for hamburgers, we came back quite late. We stumbled through the dark, taking a leak on white rocks. Inside we found our bunks and spread our sleeping bags. I remember that our heads faced an eastern wall. In that dark room my eyes closed when my father's voice broke the silence.

A faint blue light appeared through the front windows. Slowly it brightened, growing in intensity, until the entire room was suffused in a bright blue.

I could see my father bolt upright. I turned back to the windows.

Suddenly the source of the light shifted at once to the north window, and the light remained from that position illuminating the room in a weird twilight of blue and yellow and traces of red. And then it left.

I could not stop talking about what we had seen. I spoke of this for so long and so often that it is difficult now to imagine how eventually the memory of the lights began to fade, the details trailing off as those animated colors had so suddenly vanished. The lore of this episode has now been so dislodged that, only recently, it took some time to spur my father's memory of that moment long ago. I like to imagine it as a kind of visitation. The experience inverted the scene of the hunt, haunting my imagination with alien visitors looking through spacecraft glass into the little house to see a movement of bodies under sheets and deciding, no, not today: let them spread out again, and so, to their paces, let them go.

Is it possible that the visible presence of some alien and as-yet-unnamed aspect of ourselves roams the sky? It perhaps descends at vulnerable moments to awaken our curiosity. For now I shall call it the Slow Poetry in America Vision of Lights.

Awakening. What could it be, to grasp, reach, thrash out ungainly?

Summer. Dusk. I walk along limestone ridges and juniper brush, the smell of sun tan lotion and cannabis alerting me to the proximity of people, summer bathers up from the parking lot: they are on their way to the cliffs to dive and drink into the night.

The light turns pinkish blue along the horizon. Summer. I was awakening, coming to my senses only now, momentarily, to retrieve a young man in cut-off shorts carrying a beer along the escarpment's sheer cliff; a cut of rock straight down into dark water. I have no soul: I exist the same as the tiny blue juniper berries clinging to the green needle stems; like the rough bark of an oak; the glimmering surface of water while the light shifts.

Awakening. Into what or from what state into the next? The one constant: a reaching out. Where do I go? Where are the things around me that once I felt through my skin, and now see only in memory? Blond hair and brown arms; I climbed down to a thick deposit of limestone and there traced the little fossil indentations in the rock left by creatures long dead those millions of years. Boat lights sparked out in the darkening water; voices above me came suddenly with laughter; a guitar made music.

I put my feet in the water. So much time passes as though I have been sleeping. I stretch out in the dark on the rock to listen to the lapping of waves. Breath moves in my body, blood thick in my veins.

When the moon glows and the stars brighten a bit of sky with old narrative, my friends begin calling for me. My eyes are closed; I hear their voices. Slowly I stir, slip out of a dream and lose contact with myself, the person here, writing the other into awakening.

THROWING BOTTLES AT ROAD SIGNS

Jim Beavers drove his truck down the state highway between Palestine and Jacksonville. We took turns throwing empty beer bottles at road signs in time to break against the metal. The sound of glass shattering interrupted the hum of tires on asphalt and pine trees, and distant lights penetrating through the shadowy branches brightened the windshield in midnight back roads called Slow Poetry in America.

Late night evangelical voices gathered from the pines and red dirt and the thick smell of agriculture and feedlots. O Lord, the voices cried, we submit ourselves to your ways. Our bodies are small. Our minds deformed. We are prostrate unto you, dear God Jesus Christ of the Wilderness of our hearts. You died so we might die to live in you, o Christ Jesus imperishable love of eternal moon and sun that guides us with light in both night and day. For God so loved the world that he gave his loneliest only....

Slow Poetry in America urged those backwoods voices, those theologians of despair and dementia. What crazed insistence pushed those men into states of pure release, voices high-pitched nearly to the point of screaming with desire into the mothy night beer drunk and racially divided? White voices charismatically claimed pathways to God, and reinforced the alien separation of the pines and dogwoods as forlorn black communities recoiled in isolate red dirt, social disadvantage. A persuasive force was exerted in that evangelic speech, and it was thin as the Scotch-Irish lips pursed with sin in the imagination of the place. The power of that oratory remains immense, though its passion is carried in disguises of hate and apocalyptic vision.

Another empty bottle tossed into the dark through the cab window. A sound of broken glass receded into the black night behind us.

WHITE ROCK LAKE

Dallas pitched its glass and steel through a humid silvery haze. Miles of highways and subdivisions exerted the faith of its people. I grew my hair long; cut the sleeves off my t-shirts. I remember dollar movies at the Glenbrook Theater (*The World According to Garp, Clash of the Titans, Risky Business*). I remember going to prom in a black tuxedo and eating at the San Francisco Steak House, where servers presented the table an entire block of cheese.

After dancing, I drove with my girlfriend to a picnic area on White Rock Lake. We listened to the radio and felt the warmth of Slow Poetry in America on our necks and faces as the sound of traffic buzzed in the distance. I felt her thighs and the wetness in her panties increase as she rubbed against my fingers. I remember thinking it would be wrong to have sex because God would punish me. But that night I wondered, how bad could it *be* (God's wrath)? She encouraged me to take off my clothes as my body hastened into hers. The dense black sky and orange haze of streetlights with moths congealed in us. A body of feeling coheres invisibly through concentrations of will and resistance. And a great reaching, after what once seemed impossible to understand, becomes an ordinary event too rarely scrutinized, if felt as a value in self-determination.

I remember this now, my girlfriend and her big Oldsmobile, and the terrible synth-beat music of eighties radio. No separation—the environment seeps through the membrane of your feeling.

There was nothing extraordinary about our intimacy, though it seemed so then. She spread a blanket, and we lay in bluestem fields, fucking as often as possible until August, when she went away to college. That fall I would drive out to the lake many nights by myself and think of her to exhaust my loneliness. I felt like Adam, a taste of fruit in my mouth, new knowledge of my body, and nothing to do with it, alone as I was. To fill the empty space, Jim Beavers, who now had inherited his brother's red Pontiac LeMans, would pick me up and we'd 'cruise' Forrest Lane, showing off his car while looking for girls. Saturday nights the street filled with automobiles and young people. It was very *American Graffiti* in those final days of cruising culture. Parades of chrome and metal flashed by in the lit-up spectacle of North Dallas. In a parking lot we'd meet our friends: jocks, goat ropers, stoners, and freaks. Some drove 4X4 trucks, others T-top Cameros, Fieros, Trans-Ams, Firebirds, or Mavericks. We goofed around getting stoned under strip mall lights in the glowy buzz of weekend traffic.

Once, we met some prostitutes. Tight red spandex clothing hugged their brown skin. Show me your dick, one said, leaning aggressively into the car. If you ain't a cop, you'll show me your dick. We were suddenly scared (at least *I* was). I rolled up the car window; Jim Beavers pressed the gas and we sped back to the suburbs. We played basketball in garage light when we returned to his house and talked about how we'd handle ourselves *next time*. It used to be so nice to think about *next time*, all the ones to come.

GUITAR

Grass on bare feet. I played Slow Poetry in America on my Yamaha sitting by the porch alone in balmy evening air. There wasn't anything to do but to play it and pretend I was me being someone else in a kind of ongoing daydream: a dream of awakening.

The guitar sounded roundly through the neighborhood, and into the oak branches and white caliche beside St Augustine yards and the street. Someone walked by, but they were not listening to Slow Poetry in America.

In the sounds of my tuning lay a dormant hope, I think. But what do you define as hope? Maybe (probably) I just wanted to get laid and get away from scratching my frets with an awkward noise called Slow Poetry in America.

There was no school, no family: no stars or moon or trees or breeze. The hum of bats and barking owls seemed to conspire to squeeze out all but the pith of my adolescent mania. If this was lonely self-instruction in listening, wow. A deepening into myself also threatened me with disorientations toward the given criteria at hand. Those bedrock notions of family, home, and other locating forms of the every day, dissolved, or fell back behind a yearning to go beyond them. The alchemical disorganization of adolescence requires a negative adjustment to the closest aspects of oneself.

We ask how to come into ourselves? And trust no one in the transformation that involves a painful expansion of capacities and realizations of distance from the impositions of the larger social environment. Soon it had felt like I'd been turned inside out, and made myself exposed to a bent pace of imagination. And the breeze, and the heat of the late summer evening unconfined me eventually.

I renewed the careful signatures of possibility: Slow Poetry in America.

STYX

Slow Poetry in America the hidden, the submerged.
What comes to mind is a quick drifting and settling,
a determination of inexact orders.
    The whole sound of quick
  flight and figures featured:
    pet terrapin, the band Styx, lifting
  weights in summer
    nighttime garage. Sleeveless top
  exposed arms and bench
    presses cohere
  my young mind
    in the mindlessness of a new
  body awareness. Quicken
    tempo—operatic
  shifted signals, cross-beat passages
    into a future beyond.
  Alert in new salvages
    (haywire destiny) observe.

EIGHTIES

Apartheid. Iran-Contra. Desmond Tutu. Oliver North. Cap Weinberger. Nicaragua. El Salvador. Grenada. USSR. Libya. Lockerbie. *Red Dawn*. Gorbachev. Ballistic. Self-defense. Challenger. Disco. *Urban Cowboy*. Dan Quail. Cable. Music videos. Nancy Reagan's astrologer. Jody Foster. East Germany. Berlin. The Wall. 'Let's Dance.' 'Meat is Murder.' The Clash. Stevie Nicks. Vietnam vets. Homelessness. Addicts. 'This is your brain.' 'Safe Sex.' TV evangelicals. Jesse Helms. Ford Mustang. Heavy Metal. Spiked hair. Linda Ronstadt. Izod. Polo. Nukes. Spooks. Voodoo economics. Northern Ireland. North Sea. Sex Pistols. *MASH*. *Dukes of Hazard*. *Dallas*. VHS. *Top Gun*. Tom Cruise. Dan Rather. Barbara Walters. *60 Minutes*. Three-piece suits. The Hague. Camp David. 'I can't drive 55.' *Less Than Zero*. Walkman. Popped collars. Vinyl. Van Halen. Escalation. Power lunch. Power ties. Derrida. De Mann. Foucault. The burbs. *The Shining*. *Terms of Endearment*. Past lives. 'We are the World.' 'Life's a Beach.' *Apocalypse Now*. Long

Island Ice Tea. Biafra. Devo. Cape Town. Soweto.
Paul Harvey—good day?

LITTLE SLICE OF YELLOW

On a walk along the Colorado, I found a night heron roosting on a cypress root rising from the brown water. Red-eared snappers sunned on a partially submerged log of an oak nearly choked with poison ivy.

I watched the heron for some time, its little slice of yellow on regal display. A pragmatic attention held me, when suddenly, snap: it had taken a crawfish from the water. Head held upward, it swallowed the prey whole. The heron looked things over, somewhat satisfied, but cautious. Assuming her posture again, she maintained calm command of the little cypress clearing.

Slow Poetry in America the Heron.

Sometimes I stop at a little walking bridge that spans one of the tributaries of the Colorado at Barton Springs. Once, when my children were young, we hung our heads through the railings and watched coots dive in clear green water. White feet pointed up toward us; white beaks down; black bodies writhing quickly lower into water. Eventually, to my sons' delight, the birds popped up buoyantly. They'd wrestle small fish from their beaks down black throats until absorbing the little minnows completely.

Slow Poetry in America the Coots.

WHITE HEAT LIGHT FLAT LIMESTONE GLARE

Through the windshield, a stretch of Guadalupe thinned out as people lunched at El Patio and Mad Dog's and Les Amis.

Parked the car. My thin arms flipped through vinyl records at Record Exchange on the Drag. *Meat is Murder, Mirror Moves, Stop Making Sense.*

Slow Poetry in America flashed by, windows down, toward a ledge on the edge of town above the Colorado. My hand on the wheel; twilight and summer gloam.

I drank beers with Jennifer, a young woman I once knew. We sat above the city and admired our purchases as the last of the sun vanished behind us.

I yammered on about REM as she put her hand on my leg. The closer she got, the more I talked. And then I fiddled with her bra strap in the Slow Poetry in America night of cicadas buzzing in dusky heat.

Jennifer often picked me up to spend evenings at Les Amis where we would drink carafes of cheap Valpolicella, or we'd go to The Varsity to watch Italian movies, and afterwards talk about art and cinema in ways that were so new to me then.

We talked about politics, too, performing Marxist dogmas that, in a way, seemed so meaningful in the eighties, when a system of signs began tightening under Reagan and Thatcher, and their new economy of Yuppie mobility.

In the Cold War that I remember, we were all encouraged not to think about what happened *over there*. And that's what gave so many of my generation permission to take seriously what was forbidden *here*, in terms of the circulation of an underground art and poetry.

I remember the heat and sweat and June bugs, and staying up all night talking with my friends about everything. Slow Poetry in America filtered through our voices, often confused, or wrong-headed, though at times, according to our passions, we could be absolutely correct.

I remember how Jennifer insisted that I read Jean Baudrillard. I remember that we met in the stacks of the Perry Castañeda Library to argue about Hal Foster's *The Anti-Aesthetic*, and what it meant to be post-modern.

Looking all the way back it's hard to imagine that optimism. There was little money for anything.

I worked as a cook in a fast-food restaurant. The Internet didn't exist, and so we had to figure things out through word-of-mouth, or by reading a book. The coffee shops and taverns around the University of Texas were locations of information exchange.

Jennifer encouraged my capacities for learning by not putting down the far-out theories I tried on from time to time. We gave ourselves permission to look at the world, and not to be embarrassed or discouraged by what others might find either dangerous or corny.

We sat in the heat drinking beer on a limestone ledge. Slow Poetry in America, white stone, juniper, and oak. We watched the suburbs sprawl out over the Hill Country: looked at cars along the highway jammed by the intensity of commuting those far distances, from the outskirts into town and back.

OFF ROAD

Slow Poetry in America was driving along I-35 drinking beer in the rain. A plume of storm clouds spread over the flat plains between Waco and Dallas. A line of tornadoes touched down in distant pastures, and in my excitement I spilled a bottle in my lap, lost control of the car, and spun off the road into a ditch in the median.

In the rain and wind and mud I pushed the car with the help of some Latino laborers who had stopped when they saw me veer off the road. I thanked them with beer, and we all continued to our various destinations north on the Interstate.

RUBY'S BARBECUE

A ceiling fan spun in the humid air on the covered patio at Ruby's Barbecue in Austin. Across the street Blues from Antone's wailed into the parking lot. I drank a beer under mothy bulbs. Look back all that way to Slow Poetry in America. A slim young man in jeans; a white shirt; sneakers; glasses too big for his face.

Car lights and orange streetlights illuminated Guadalupe Street. Groups of people walked by. Laughter. A sudden voice, a phrase: 'No Shit?' And then the sounds were reabsorbed into the general commotion of traffic and music; the electric buzzings and squeaky door hinges animated the little patio where I sat with a book by William Carlos Williams.

It was not enough to imagine, but to press thought against impulse, and to experience imagination as both wonder and inquiry. The red wheelbarrow, the delicious plums, pressed back on subjective experience, not with objective fact, but conceptual act. Words themselves are not enough; nor the believed certitude of experience: not even the subjective perception activates the relationship to the object. An abstraction of the relationship is inevitable, although the surface is deceptively plain.

Moths fluttered unruly. A loud harmonica pierced the field of automobiles.

'It is the mystery of the past which monsters, grotesques, beasts combined with the human, truly signify—gentle animal associations distorted by the invasions of night—and not a debased instinct whose reliance is necessarily upon oppression and fear. The earth is black and it is there: only art advances.'

But what is it to 'advance'—truly? Those creatures whose forms left shapes in the limestone walls of the University of Texas where I studied so many long hours—what advance did those ancient mollusks and clams gain through their transposition into sediment? Ammonites and worm tubes passed through coastal waters that flooded far inland. Oyster and heart urchin possessed active potential in that pre-human slime and damp. See those creatures now time-stamped on Parlin Hall. By their examples E. M. Cioran is right: 'Any profound impression is voluptuous or funereal—or both at once.'

Sticky skin; sweat thick on my forehead.

Brute facts, the ordinary reality of my self: these were hammered out against a language of excavation and soil. Advance toward Awakening. Not self as subjective trap, but one who populates the field of a larger attention.

I ordered a brisket sandwich and potatoes. Pushed into contradictions, pathways that promised new features of a hidden landscape. I look back at myself then exposed as one of those mute moths in the light. Memory can't be trusted—neither can one's optimistic insight to the past, or the past self, re-imagined, in the disorienting drift of prose. What comes to mind can be seen in violation to all that does not. The topic of self, at any rate, can only work as an excuse to dive into the dark, and hope the water is deep enough to submerge any egoistic attempt to remember the past, unless there is the pressure of self-critical investigation.

APPLICABLENESS

'Hear me,' said Charles Olson. 'Not referential, but inner inherence / Not learning, but applicableness.' Slow Poetry in America gives body to the many sequences of perception as we shape it. The shape of one's forms of life takes on new contours, going forward and looking back, listening closely to patterns that suggest 'inner inherence.' Our lives enter narratives that crisscross with others into sudden, and brief, moments of arrival. I walk out to buy toothpaste or fruit, speak to the Asian at the fruit stand, or briefly exchange a glance with a Greek as we navigate icy sidewalks. We catch each other's eyes—and then vanish. The outer references, the shapes of things, are reformed, distorted, reassigned to the unfolding of an impersonal form by which our substance thrives.

DESERT MUSIC

In 1992, I studied Arabic at a madrassa in Sana'a, and then moved to Hodeidah to work as a teacher. In the streets at Bab al-Yemen were many suqs and people seeking goods and food, and there were moneychangers providing riyals for my dollars. I dipped bread in spicy beans. I remember rolling blackouts and kerosene lanterns. I remember speaking to vendors in Arabic for the first time. I remember a pace of life before the Internet and laptops and plugging in. I remember long drives through mountain roads in a shared taxi, while the driver conducted prolonged discourses with fellow passengers as the dry mountain villages flashed by us. I remember a wrecked jeep and the body of a man on the hood. I remember my feet in the Red Sea, floating in the salty water, and how warm it was in December. I remember hot, sweet tea. I remember climbing stone steps of the castle at Wadi Dhahr. I remember a man who was chained to a tree in the village of Wadi Dhahr, and that people said he was crazy. I remember visiting friends in distant cities.

I remember Hunt Oil and the CIA and Marines at the American Embassy (where there was beer). I remember reading Stendhal between classes in the afternoon. I remember my roommate who came from Seattle, and how he moved to Tangiers eventually, and then later to Iraq during the Bush years. I remember sunlight in a blue kitchen drinking coffee, and chewing qat on the roof of my building. I remember makeshift shacks and Somali beggars on the street. I remember refugee camps and an Ethiopian café where I drank coffee outdoors on a patio watching television. I remember when it rained and the streets flooded. I remember Michael Jackson and Pepsi. I remember Turkish buildings on the boardwalk in Hodeidah. I remember the kindness of many people in Sana'a and Hodeidah and Taiz and Ibb. I remember that it seemed upon leaving America I had exited a bubble. I remember how strange things in America appeared from my newly imposed distance. I remember reading in *Newsweek Magazine* about mujahidin soldiers in Bosnia. I remember how it felt to be foreign in American skin.

SANA'A

Slow Poetry in America sat on a bench in Tahrir Square in Sana'a. I was eating a croissant—a rare treat—when the man beside me spoke. The traffic buzzed around us. In the distance mountains rose dryly above the city. Men in long zeinas and jambiyahs walked along the park paths. One man offered pictures with his falcon.

The man who shared my bench told me he was a teacher from Iraq working in Yemen. You're American, aren't you, he said. Yes, I said. American.

He ate a sandwich but seemed distracted. He was not dressed in Yemeni garb, but wore a cheap suit and dirty white shirt.

At the time, Bill Clinton had ordered air strikes on Baghdad. The Iraqi looked at me earnestly, asking that I speak to my president to stop the suffering in his country. He could find no work there and so, like me, took a job in an outpost in one of the poorest countries of the world.

Later, in Hodeidah, one of my Somali colleagues was similarly confused by the US intervention in

Somalia. Why are you at war with us, he asked, earnestly searching my eyes for a reaction? At the time, Somali refugees came in great numbers to the Yemeni coast.

When I arrived in Sana'a, the first thing I noticed was a strong smell in the air like burning plastic and diesel and animals. I sought out the maze-like streets of Bab al-Yemen and enjoyed the company of my friends in the qat suqs and coffee shops of the city. I could see America, at last (or I glimpsed what it might mean *to see* in this specific sense), and I understood that I had escaped a vast membrane of ignorance and self-protection.

INSIDE SEEING

There was an image in my mind of what I wanted to be. Look to see what can't be seen any longer, to release possession of a child, a boy—the young man marked by what limitations of imagination? The objects of a room: glass on a table, teakettle, spatula, a dirty frying pan. Through a window came afternoon traffic and people moving along shop fronts. Plain. Physical. Warmth of feeling. When you see what you see it's inside your seeing, how the image settles its quickening to your nature. Slow Poetry in America pressed close to me. Dust blew up on Shara al-Sana'a as truck fumes sprayed the air along afternoon sidewalks outside shops with no distracting advertisements. Slow Poetry in America held my hand in the afternoon suqs and in the convivial spaces of dinner. Slow Poetry in America disbanded in my whiteness an alien comfort of sensations newly imagined. To wander inside yourself and there find distortions. It's your face but not you as you were, but are. Not to be but become other in a reaching to know the fragment traces. The high old city was driven beyond its walls. Bab Al-Yemen thrived, mud-baked, a living thing spilling from ancient form. Men at a table with tea; the racket of French lorries and fumes and dust; my face with a barber mirrored in a patchwork of bright image.

TIHAMA

Afternoon prayers in Tihama village. Two children tossed coins under palm trees and a radio pulsed. Donkeys pulled banana carts. I shared egg sandwiches with kids who smelled like metal and sand. Men prayed. I leaned on the Peugeot taxi, watching ants patrol rocks at my feet. Not everyone spread a rug. Some shared cigarettes. One praised the mountain view. Hood hot, lime green. Villagers in a field loaded things to be carted from the terraced mountainside. Our driver peeled a peach. Amriki? Franci? my companions asked. Espani, I said, the car motoring a quiet turn of mountain while one man crawled to the back crying, *al-kibdah*, his side on fire, and two more hours to hospital. In Sana'a, I ordered food. Walked the blacked out back streets beside blue-lit shops.

AL-YOUM

Met expats for brunch at the Taj Sheba hotel. Scooped fresh fruit and fancy desserts. Eggs benedict. Curries. Western coffee. Then back to school, listening to children who played with radio dials and their parents' Arabic in a cool late breeze as I digested to the quiet of their evening.

The first time I spoke with confidence I ordered a bowl of *fasoolya*—a spicy bean dish—and more to impress friends added '*basal*'—onions ordered simply. Then when the food was late I looked at the man and said, '*al-Youm*؟'—today? The limited vocabulary stranded me in self-conscious shame. I had puffed up behind an access through new language, and the insipid weight of empire reinforced an advance of attitude. The comfortable habitation in white skin that had been a given in the States now no longer could be enforced. I stood as financial entity—an extension of economy and force that like some webbing stranded my actions by a sticky program of defense. No matter how at home I attempted to make the place, there was no escaping who I was or what my nationality signified so conclusively. There is no ease or comfort; a deep dissatisfaction with speech and body code, the manipulated tendencies of belief, interfere with self-insight. The mutability of perception, and its translation into action, confounds attempts to look inward, to know what I feel, even as what I feel to be true is traced out in quick glimpses, internalizations of specific environments and moods.

Later, I remember sitting under an awning drinking tea as plastic bags shifted in the sand, waiting for a ride out of town. Somber notes accompanied the call to prayer, and the fumes of traffic filled the air around me. Makeshift tarps provided shade to merchants and their wares of fruit and other goods.

TAIZ

Goats in ancient sunlight baahing
Greet our breakfast beans and bread;
We spread low under suq awnings
Where a man with a monkey mends
A basket; observe the primate
Expression, withdrawn, primitive,
Mask bartering animal
Charisma; people gather;
Behold the chiseled lines long
Weathered on the man's face; Egyptian
Arabic, and French words intercede
Our exchange in dust and tea
Beside the falconer meaning
To pry for coin; and give way

ELEGIAC

Something elegiac pushes through my writing. I recognize it—follow the long and lyrical apprehensions and cascading forms of thought cohering as Slow Poetry in America. The relations of men to their bodies were different in Yemen. There was affection for words, ideas, and the physical close charms of breath and flesh. A grave pressure exacts certain demands on my attention. I look at my words and think, loosen up! Beyond the varying topographies and the constellated, prism-like shields of personality I seek a connective dimension of memory in the quicksilver moments of cohering form. I see myself as a child in my father's truck; I see the blond boy in a world of suburban plenty; I see the ordinary privilege of life extracted for me, and think about its consumption. I look through time to find thin tracings, the young man reading Marx and Baudrillard in cafés, or the one with Whitman and William Carlos Williams, inky stains in an air-conditioned library. I find the forms of my children and use them to understand the unsayable things that resist symbolization. Even now they rest, midafternoon in winter, crisp light intensified by its reflection in icy snow, streaming through a window. They sleep, feverish, under blankets on a couch unconscious to the world except as it is revealed in their dreaming. What I find is a resistance to a shaping of memory and narrative. The pieces are disordered, the impressions so tender and subtle they may not exist at all. The traumatic force of life presses confirmation of one's senses. I shift the contents over and over again. The bomb threatens the temperament of childhood, or a father's anger lies close to the surface of violence, or terror flashes with codified success into the global present. The World War shaped my parents' generation just as Vietnam and the manic release of archaic ritual formed the background of consciousness in the 1960s. The Alberta oil fields threaten precious prairie land and river deltas, and perhaps will irrevocably destroy our climates, while coal extraction adds millions of tons of carbon into the atmosphere every year. The New World is threatened by accountant scrutiny, and political motive since 1492 has been shaped to extract, deform, maim, and haunt. The intermittent play of wonder and terror, of delight and fear, draws out the personal from the shared concerns of cultural memory. When does memory intervene—and make it new? Slow Poetry in America asserts a little point of resistance. Its temporary allegiances flower beautifully forth, and fade into the obdurate and obscure, stone-like, a little flake or filament, gone.

KESTREL

The Interstate splits two directions: northeast and northwest. A kestrel clings to a wire, and wiry ribbons break the horizon. Cellphone towers. A narrative dissolves beyond description: it demands powerful scrutiny and slow, prolonged, internalization.

My hand steadies the wheel as the sky and headlights unsteady the horizon. Moonlight in the misty breeze. The provisory instant requires careful steps into the conceptual to align with the varying cadences of experience. But thought, too, offers a cataract perspective, a rough water passage toward increased clarifications that, finally, weaken, evaporate.

Slow Poetry in America the highway signals the grainy fields of Nebraska. Trains deliver loads of crushed coal to power plants from Wyoming to Texas, and beyond. Resource contraction is inevitable; new forms of technology to fix the situation are unlikely. Slow Poetry in America sinks inward. Buckle up for a ride. To see across the prairies, look out through kestrel eyes.

A PLAN

It's tempting to think there's a plan when there isn't. I try to peer into my life from different vantage points, to create a brief illusion of my former selves. Sometimes only a little flicker of light comes out of all that dark possibility. One's affection, one's desire, appears against an immense background that absorbs thoughts and feelings that once had such a hold. I found I could be persuaded into action quite easily, producing erratic shifts of energy and values to encourage the habitations of new drives and willful self-summaries: new interior maps created to harmonize with some half-formed dream of what I was or was supposed to be. I somehow felt I controlled where I would go and what I might become. I didn't quite realize what little wherewithal I possessed. I thought I held the key, but my pockets were empty. The dirt farm Depression-era crush of the past trellised behind me like cans tied to the cars of newlyweds. No maps and no encouragements. No one to dissuade bad decisions. Cheap oil and easy resources—no moral system—made my actions palpable. There I stand perfectly naked, with everything before me. I put gas in my car and I drove it away far west. Coal shipped from Wyoming lit my evenings, and I read about a Cadillac Desert and the End of Nature, but did nothing to alter my consumption. I now try to look through myself as though some kind of time machine illuminates the past. I can't say what brought me here is genetic or familial; I can't say if it was social or political: I think something environmental, and therefore fundamentally moral, wagered on the success or failure of my remote actions. Even 'environment' and 'moral' resist the pressed conditions I seek to describe, how interactions with food and resources shape actions (the outer forms that express belief). Decisions of consumption—of food, energy, information—transform the organism and alter situations often, as we see, irrevocably. This is not to express guilt of any kind, but to acknowledge the absurd tensions in an environment often disguised as personal motive. How do you hone a semblance of fealty in a place that dissolves by your touch? Slow Poetry in America, I ask you.

MOON CAMP

I had heard about the Willamette National Forest and wanted to travel out of the valley of golf course grass where I had been living (the rich Willamette Valley specialized, by the 1990s, in growing seeds for tournament greens). I looked out across the acres of farmland and saw snowy peaks in the distance of the mighty Cascade Range.

I also heard it was quite easy for anyone to go camping in those formidable mountains thick and piney green with great densities of Douglas fir.

In those days before Google, I had to go to Corvallis to find a map. I traced out a route through Lebanon and Sweet Home (names that still excite my appetite for that country).

You had to drive a couple of hours up out of the valley into the Cascades. I followed US-20 until turning onto a narrow National Park road. My Beetle crawled up the mountain pass toward an advantageous trail where I'd hike into the mountains. After I had pulled over I took out my gear: a tent, sleeping bag, some matches, water, food. I found a little place an hour or so later and built my camp.

I was reading Jaime de Angulo, about the first peoples on the West Coast. I cracked a beer, put my feet up, and took notes in a field book.

As it grew dark I built a fire, and felt the good summer cold of the mountains.

That night I poked my head out of the tent to go piss. Saw my breath in the moonlight and the moon winked bright silver through the atmosphere.

Some say it's overly sentimental to write about the tired cliché of the sweetness of our moon. And perhaps they're right. But it forms such a prominent feature in our lives, one too prime to ignore. Poets so often make pronouncements anyway that mean very little. They press against the limits of what they know and feel in order to strike a semblance of accuracy. Slow Poetry in America the Moon glides across the sky and is okay with things down here. There are many fashions, many ins and outs. But if you call the moon into a poem you must be very careful. Some abuse the moon and reduce it to a thin semblance. A poem is a wild thing, and must be tended with great caution. Once you write about the moon you must understand what has been evoked. Likewise, if the moon is banished from a poem, know what dark humor abides in orbits of stricter possibility.

PORTLAND

Slow Poetry in America stalked me in coffee shops and taverns in Portland, Oregon.

I felt like someone trying to be something I could not figure out. The rain fell cold on me as I walked to Powell's Books, and sometimes the rain turned to snow and back to rain again. Mt Hood stood out snowy above the city skyline, and in the afternoon I would go down to the Willamette and watch the barges pass under bridges at Burnside or Broadway.

I read the Black Mountain poets and got tangled up in what I thought I understood but didn't. I had to reach out beyond myself into an uncomfortable place of objectivity, following the projective mode. But frequently I lost track despite my best efforts, and I was exposed, withheld from myself in a mind-wandering daze. Words got away from me and I lost sight of them in that drippy city.

How ordinary: I was obsessed with the ever-present need to write, read, write again, type. In coffee shops, I wrote words with Ron Silliman's *Tjanting* beside me. Sentence after sentence of his dense books excited my curiosity for words. I followed his endless thicket of language, lost in a narrow syntax of symbolic possibility. Language came magnified beyond its ability to signify the human capacity to think or feel. This was odd and informing, and I let the words settle thickly as I read and re-read across those outer folds of attention. The materiality struck me as something corrosive and also inviting. The overlap and animation of writing generated narratives of pure will under-mined by a savage and uprooted insistence of words.

FACTS

The humid night increases. Sweat. Slow Poetry in America squeezes into the room uncomfortably, large as a continent of mud. Breath, smoke. The boozy afterglow of getting high. Like something ghostly Pascal said: the accident of being in time set against the closure of eternity, the no time without pace. A drift of attention into the knotty flesh and fatty expanses of pleasure. A wetness on the balcony. Thin droplets of rain or mist, yes, the mist. Body against body because there's no time. Damp air and party lights dimmed. A page to become blank by the ink that makes it. To write out the facts and substitute with an ecstatic blankness. Writing erases the most intimate, until there's nothing. Not even an empty page competes with the weight of words, and the prescient force of their powers to dissolve.

READING PHILIP WHALEN

I discovered Philip Whalen's poetry in the late spring of 1995 while living in San Francisco. A close friend of mine, Anselm Berrigan, noticed certain similarities in my work that reminded him of Whalen. At the time, much of his writing was out of print, so I was lucky to find several used books in various Mission and Noe Valley bookstores. The first I picked up was *The Kindness of Strangers*, a collection of poems written from the mid 1960's through the early '70's. As a young poet, new to the West Coast, I was unfamiliar with much of the writing produced during the San Francisco Renaissance, that vibrant moment where Jack Spicer, Robert Duncan, Lew Welch, George Stanley, Joe Dunn, Joanne Kyger, and so many others created a West Coast practice distinct from Allen Ginsberg, Jack Kerouac, and the Beats. While Whalen is often associated with the Beats—Joanne Kyger, in an August 28, 1959, letter to Michael Rumaker calls him 'the best of the so called beat poets'—his long life in the West, and his prolonged attention to Zen religious practices in California, indicates an extensive connection to that geographic region. In temperament and thought, he is singular, and resists easy classification, anyway. Whalen has the felicitous, upbeat swing of a jazz musician in his writing, built on a practice of study in religion, philosophy, history, and much more.

On first reading Whalen's poetry I was drawn into the movement and range of his lines while simultaneously being thrown off balance. Associative leaps led from the particular details of experience and perception to the distant echoes and ephemera of his memory. I came to understand that he applied the pressure of thought against the mind to organize coherent poems from dissimilar compositional moments, located variously in the physicality of place, or the immaterial projection of memory and imagination. The sound in the work conjoined with the poetic imagination to clarify a voice that also diverges, pulling the outside in while pushing internal habits, fetishes, desires, and interests to the poem's surface. Whalen adhered to strict observation. Rather than taking a cohering, progressive approach to the social surface, he structured the details of his perceptions in a way that could present a conceptualized strangeness. He found a means to express the mystery of daily experience through the equally mysterious process of perception. In a 1972 poem entitled 'Weather Odes,' he writes:

With a head full of sunlight
What's killing you now?

No patience to sit and watch the ivy grow
No patience with sleep
Exhausted by a band of mare's tails
Moving down from the north
Right across the sky from west to east
(West is the beginning of Ocean)

In this brief passage about simply watching clouds pass through the sky, the voice of the poem remarks on a tension in the very impatience of the movement. The imagination lingers with the clouds, describing them as ivy or a band of mare's tails—a colloquialism for cirrus clouds—while the voice invoking the perception is self-critical, showing an uncomfortable sense of the movement, as though time was being wasted. It is as if the voice is incapable of maintaining the cliché of the poet, whose head is in the clouds, while at the same time maintaining interest enough to remain there, still revealing the clouds in a language that offers expansion of process and awareness, although the writer is impatient with himself, or even with the knowledge of these parsed events of perception, self, language, or projection into phenomenal possibility. The movement of the stanzas opens into the 'beginning of Ocean,' placing the reader beyond the poet's personal moment of internal anxiety and listlessness while connecting vast geographical landscapes within a frame of perception both narrow and broad in the topography of the poem. Later on we read:

A head full of discontented screams,
Roars, motor noises, rockets,
Extraterrestrial ray guns, dogs,
Chickens, carpenters, noon whistle (all the way
  from Stinson Beach,
    population 84, an air-raid siren, just imagine!)
The blue sky clabbering up to rain?

The impatience of the previous stanza gives way to specific annoyances. But again, the details of 'discontented screams, roars, motor noises' detail the landscape. The mind takes interest in the distractions, giving substance and position to the terrestrial landscape as clouds grow heavy with the possibility of rain. Details of place converge to form a mini-drama with the tension of the poet's restlessness and distractions. Due to the attention to detail and the care of the language, this drama of distraction holds the poem within a field of widening suggestion as the overtones reverberate to reveal something to the reader of process and attention even within a moment of personal annoyance. The mysterious humor of the lines is formed by the listing of nouns that both comment on the moment and send out echoes of a larger process, a process the poet himself, in the specific moment, is momentarily incapable of hearing. The poem moves outwards to us through the very details that prevent the speaker from being left undisturbed. That a poem has been made at all from this suggests the nuanced positions Whalen seeks to identify in the process of poetic creativity. He allows the poem to reveal the thought and mood of the poet within a greater social and subjective context. The poet is both irrelevant and necessary within the world of sight, sound, and event, for he must be there to record.

The poem, however, might reveal things that escape initial observation. The poem actually hears more than the voice can express. In the juxtaposition of tone and object, the language lifts out from the speaker, from Whalen's mind, both revealing that particular mind, and then some.

PHILIP WHALEN II

Whalen, at his greatest, draws out something larger than his own mind, although thought as it bears on imagination, is key. There are multiple possibilities of consciousness working either with or against the other. A poem can sometimes lift up just to have the rug pulled out from under it in a kind of deadpan humor. At other times, the placement of objects shifts by the act of his perception of them. Whalen pieces together a dense world made more explicit by dynamic acts of observation. It is dense because he complicates it through a self-aware presence, as though projection alters experience, for what he sees is not so important as how things are perceived in the poem. His concerns with the processes of the mind and perceptive possibilities and limitations recall Gertrude Stein, an early influence on his creative development. Her narrative influence was immense—and Whalen's poems, while often registering a meditative or contemplative mood of thought, often formally reveal themselves as narrative. The sense of linguistic play, the often-contradictory humor, the formal experimentation, and the sensitive attention paid to the process of attention are just some of the correlations in their writing. But there are other similarities of structure. Whalen often uses narrative in his poetry to convey a sense of place, time, and drama. His large collection of early poems, *On Bear's Head*, has the thickness of a novel, and the poems seem to be composed of fragments or journal entries that are placed in time by the date of composition following each poem. Like Stein's plays and portraits, Whalen's poetry uses language to set up certain dramatic expectations that he continually challenges and dismantles. In 'Composition as Explanation,' Stein writes, 'The only thing that is different from one time to another is what is seen and what is seen depends upon how everybody is doing everything.... Nothing changes from generation to generation except the thing seen and that makes a composition.' In 'Portraits and Repetition,' she further clarifies the relationship of generations of people to the world: 'But the strange thing about the realization of existence is that like a train moving there is no real realization of it moving if it does not move against something and so that is what a generation does it shows that moving is existing.' Whalen's writing takes these insights to 'existence' and adjusts his writing as a kind of instrument of keen notation, and 'shows that moving is existing.' A way to appreciate this is seen in the stance both writers take toward composition. I do not mean to reduce Whalen to a single artistic source, for there are many others—like William Carlos Williams, whom he met as a student at Reed College. Whalen tends to record the physical and mental states interacting in diverse environments, while Stein processed in new terms a formal act of invention and arrangement. The reliance both he and Stein have on composition as the organizing field of perception is important to consider.

Whalen's generation was the first to inherit Stein and make use of her fundamentally ground-breaking moves. Like Stein, Whalen composes 'portraits,' and he continually makes depictions of the phenomenal world. The strong narrative element in his poetry, along with the play-like structure of his verse, also recalls Stein's poetic plays, read more like poems than theater. With Whalen, any system of reading can miss something of importance. The absurdity, or much of what seems simplistic on the surface, hides a more complex and thoughtful tension below the poem. There is also the added dimension of subjective concerns in Whalen's work that Stein did not address in her own. Where she is fundamentally social and material, Whalen is religious and spiritual.

WHALEN'S SELF-PORTRAITS

In an early collection, *Memoirs of an Interglacial Age*, there are two self-portraits that reveal something of Whalen's process. In 'Self-Portrait, from Another Direction,' he writes:

> Tuned in on my own frequency
> I watch myself looking
> Lying abed late in the morning
> With music, thinking of Y

These opening lines tell us almost all we need to know in order to get at the kernel of Whalen's work. His ability to observe himself in the action of observing, and to put this across in a poem, is key—and shows a connection to Stein. But the difference is that Whalen, in this case, puts himself at the center as subject rather than someone or something else. The action of observing and the varying states of awareness revealed through composition are the concerns of the poem. In the second stanza we read:

> I think what is thinking
> What is that use or motion of the mind that
> Compares with a wink, the motion of the belly

Beside the highway
Young bullock savages the lower branches
of a big cedar tree

The self-consciousness in this poem processes the fundamental prejudice of Western dualism. Whalen answers his own question in its framing. The 'use of motion of the mind' is to reveal itself, seeing parts of a self's complexity and flux that has been divided in the West since Descartes. He then moves his attention briefly away from his subjective experience to the 'young bullock beside the highway,' that either gives the self in the poem a frame or reference, or functions as an extension of self through the self-aware perception of the mind. The perception originates in him. He questions the distance between things and the gaps formed in a creative formulation of being. Due to the juxtaposition of these lines the poem suggests that external things form a part of him due to the intimate correlation of mind and phenomena processed through the self. The relationships between the mind, self, perceptive process, and the applied pressures of external phenomena are tightly woven with a hyper-conscious awareness of language as medium of the will. Unlike Stein's, Whalen's poetry is often more concretely directed in deliberate ways toward statements of subjective complexity. Whalen's observations come out of talismanic-like objects, in a spiritual web of human complicity, where the mystery of existence is pieced together, briefly, in provisory forms. Stein meets the object and composes upon the material surface pragmatically and psychologically. For Whalen, a sense of pragmatism is also necessary to understand:

THOUGHT IS NOT SWIFT!
perhaps the mind is slower than this pencil,
  its rate of motion nearer that of the heartbeat—
moving slower than the head which turns
  not as quick as a wink

It is the impulse to live and the will driving the self forward that inhabits the center of this poem. This can be said of Whalen's other writing, too. The ability to think against thought, to listen to the larger potential complexities of the human organism, and to provide the release of this understanding through language is necessary to comprehend the difficult flux of Whalen's self-depositing aspects. Something about the process of composition allows both Whalen and Stein to show broad and difficult constructions of being through the swiftness of the image montage. Whalen's poetry questions more than it presents, pulls back before offering any answer. His drive, or will, provides the necessary cohesion for a cosmological rather than a strictly social presentation of self. Later, he challenges conventional objectivity and empiricism:

POSSIBLE TRUE STATEMENTS ABOUT A
REAL PIECE OF SANDSTONE

Now it is here.
Now it is falling
Now it is there.
which we agree upon ...
What comes next?
The landslide has revealed
The bones of Adam protruding from the soil
A bronze door into Magic Land
Z. really *was* sore at me seven years ago in
Hollywood, which is the reason Sandra never
returned my umbrella,—I see it all now ...

Behind the empirical domain of objective reality exists an historical prism of personal and cosmological significance. The humor and surprise we encounter open the poem to aspects of memory and magic. Stein's pragmatism stops at the question: what *does* come next? Whalen answers with absurdities that double as possibilities in his poetic landscape. He confronts the historical imagination through memory to address the already complex ontology alluded to earlier in the poem. But this historical dimension further represents a function of the poetic will as it pieces together more than the observable. Whalen takes leaps into fissures of thought unobtainable by materialist plunge. As the poem develops, he looks at himself within nature's borders and determines it inadequate for knowing his internal states:

Rain/wind bulging the window
An Absolute, i.e. what we think of as
'an Absolute,' 'Force,' 'NATURE'
know nothing of my love, my mind

Having reached out into the external world, Whalen acknowledges the limitations imposed by nature. Knowledge differentiates himself from external phenomena. There exist thoughts, feelings, will, love, memory, and many other possibilities underneath his skin just as the rocks earlier hid ancient archeological potentials of knowledge. By the end of the poem, Whalen acknowledges the power of language and the process of composition as the talismanic act of understanding:

> Any word you see here defies all fear doubt
>   destruction ignorance &
>   hatefulness
> All the impossibilities unfavorable chance or luck
> It will have overcome all my strength (the total
>   power of a raging
>   maniac
>   self-hypnotized berserk missing one arm part
>   of the entrails
>   exposed
>   running with incredible speed)
> Superhuman force,   an exorbitance—
>   slingstone hurled at a
>   tangent to the circle
>   in which it lately whirled
>   zipping off
>   in high-speed parabola
> Into the mirror (NOW showing many men)
>   all of them 'I'

The processes of composition defy the internal

emotional terrain of the person. This concept of 'I' represents a multiplicity of potential governed by will, nature, emotion, and thought thinking against itself through the language of poetic composition. Language, as the production of body meeting the mind in response to pressure perceived in the West as external and internal, becomes the unifying force through which diverse subjective elements meet. Although Whalen reaches for mythic self-revelation through the word, he captures the evasiveness and uncertainty of perception's role in knowledge. And while it is his will to be revealed through the process of poetry, he struggles with the given formulations of how we know in the West.

'SELF-PORTRAIT SAD'

In 'Self-Portrait Sad 22:ix:58,' Whalen takes himself as subject in all of its varying complexities, with the additional burden of emotional experience. This is a poem about self-acceptance. His thematic concerns of mind, body, and perception remain central to the piece, but the emotional element further complicates the poem, giving it a difficult interiority not as readily evident in the other self-portraits. I suppose one could go through this poem and comment on the added dimension the emotional elements have on an already difficult text. I have discussed many of the philosophical aspects of Whalen's work in 'Self-Portrait, from Another Direction.' Perhaps Lew Welch put it best in a letter to Whalen dated September 2, 1957:

> You have the curious ability to make one think that a mind has been slowed down, or speeded up, until perception is going at the exact pace of things. The impression is like a stroboscope on a hi-fi .... What happens [to the image] is the important thing, let someone with nothing else to do

figure out the why. It be won't there, then anyway. As a poem of self-acceptance and self-pity, 'Self-Portrait Sad' presents a more vulnerable side of Whalen's ability as a poet. The poem is transformative and regenerative in its shamanic scope, and its endeavor to heal.

At last I realize my true position: hovering face
down above the
world
(At this point the Pacific Coast of
The United States)
A second rate well finished nothing too much
wrong with it but
not too interesting.

He positions himself from above, as though he were a bird observing the American coast below. These lines also reveal a person new to a place, as though the very strangeness of being new and unfamiliar with place imposes a distance between the observer and the landscape. In September 1957, Whalen moved to Newport, Oregon, to work as Circuit Court Bailiff for Ben Richard Anderson, who had been appointed Circuit Court Judge for Lincoln County. Whalen would remain in relative isolation for two years in this small fishing and logging village situated on the Oregon coast. His loneliness is certainly the reason for the sad tone of the poem. But his sadness is self-mocking, too:

> & now the tree's cut down
>   Oh, well
>   I was never good at throwing
>   rocks to knock down
>   Pods from it anyway, horsechestnuts
>   Cold calsomine smell, solid chunks of brown
>   watered-silk inside
> To contemplate
>   or decorate with a pocket knife
> DOTE   DOTE   DOTE.

The ability to observe the self with humor in times of stress and isolation serves Whalen's poetry well, and shows this to be one of his greatest strengths. His range and tone are widespread. The ontological and spiritual aspects of his poetry can suddenly take quick shifts into the absurd or self-mocking. The thought and drive of the poem often doubles back, putting the original emphasis of the poem into question. The moves Whalen makes in his writing are calculated, through the daily practices of Zazen, to confound and question the intentions of the poem. This balance of keen philosophical acumen and self-humor allows the poems to reach out into the world of things with authority, while the depths of Whalen's internal solitude are revealed through this process of listening. It is about listening to himself listening to the world. And when one is sad, when the heart is broken, it is also open. It is open for growth and change. The perceptions are heightened as the world shimmers in its magnanimity. The language of the poem itself is luminous with a colloquial life traced out of childhood memory, and the rural surroundings of Oregon, Whalen's childhood home:

There is a boardinghouse
Far far away
Where they serve hash & beans
Every Saturday

O how those boarders yell
When they hear that dinnerbell
O how the boarders yell
Far far away.

The sad and playful yearning of this song echoes

with sentimental longing while rejoicing in the provocative English of the American West. Whalen rarely lets you forget where he is situated. Coastlines are mentioned, the location of mountains is given, and descriptions of landscape and city appear throughout his writing. He places himself in a way quite opposite of Stein, who examines the detail of place to the point of cubist abstraction. Observation seeks to make sense of place, emotion, and being by allowing a sense of freedom into the complexities and restrictions of the world. Whalen is able to step out and look from the distance and also to occupy the closer ranges of detailed perception. By the end of 'Self-Portrait Sad,' he has made a peace with himself and the new place where he will live out the next two years. He identifies with a seabird, writing:

> You are the ones walking around inside
>   your shells, I soar
> Face down high above the shore & sea
>   Ho ho, *skreak*, &c.
>   Come live on salmon & grow
>   wise!

Whalen makes the shamanic transformation into

the nature of a bird that will provide him strength, nourishment, and wisdom. The process gives him awareness while listening to his immediate landscape, echoes of past memory, historical, and spiritual aspects of place and self. The broken heart and the sharpened mind meet as the 'kettle-logic' of process mediates these diverse elements through a colloquial voice. The voice carries its past and present, the future becoming the possibility of expression through poetic intervention.

NEW YEAR'S 1995

Anselm and I dropped acid New Year's Eve. When we set out from his place through the park, the air warped and glossed our vision. Giant eucalyptus branches had been blown down by an earlier storm. The mighty glory of Slow Poetry in America had come on in the mordant afterglow of the drug.

When we arrived at Darrin's south of Golden Gate Park, the city sparked and then settled into a slow, unctuous density. The houses peaked with creamy thickness as moonlight scoured the eaves and windows facing the Bay. Car lights presented thick globs of orange; the colors of each passing vehicle refracted with spontaneous billowing waves of motion: red, navy, mauve. Yellow moon, silver moon, a spume of greasy light poured from Darrin's window, and we climbed the narrow stairway to his apartment.

Someone presented me with a glass of whiskey. The marvelous glowing feeling I had was amplified tremendously. Sitting at the kitchen table, John generously passed around a beautiful pink pipe. When

I took a hit the room expanded: it released colorful sparks, absorbing the entire space. And then the ceiling seemed as if to open entirely, and a mud-like creature stood out over the entire peninsula, bending under the starry sky.

The next morning I woke up to a new year of Slow Poetry in America. At 6 a.m. the luxurious light of San Francisco carried the city to my eyes.

I don't remember getting home, though Anselm led me there, worried I'd finally done serious damage to my brain. Next day he came by and we went to see a movie in Japan Town by Claude Van Damme.

Just the other day I saw Anselm for the first time in five years. He was playing with his daughters Sylvie and June when I arrived at the park near his house on East 4th. We talked about many things over the next few days, catching each other up with our lives. For a while we were content to be alone with Slow Poetry in America at The Ramble in Central Park, where red wing blackbirds, finches, and sparrows flitted spontaneously in the new warmth of spring. We're in our forties now—a long way from San Francisco. But still trying to 'figure it out.' His patient, thoughtful press into imagination and language inspires me to relocate attention in the dream-work. To compare and compose, reoriented by the warmth of friendship.

THE KETTLE LOGIC OF THE DREAM-WORK

First is grinding certitude. Each word corresponds with an action in the mind of the person in submission to a poem. Next comes a resentment in the act as the material folds back against the long-sought-after Awakening: you do not see as it was foretold; remain aloof and inert from animal senses; feign improper prejudices to barter for your gain. A man accosts you in the streets and hits you, and cuts your lip. This man is nobody, and you bleed. Later your friends will laugh, and a careful order you had constructed disappears. No beauty can suffice in the awkward drift of the dream-work. Awkward, violent dispatches of image threaten to overtake your potential: first it rains, and then it shines; it's too hot, and then too cold. The Pacific's luster darkens. Damp air cuts your throat. You step boldly out but don't have the social presentations. Self-doubt gnaws at your every word. In the kettle logic of the dream-work you suffer instability of fortune. Slow Poetry in America looks back to you through a temporal existence you hardly understand. Dissipate.

Sleep. Blink awake to thick banks of bougainvillea, so disastrous and fetching. The poem cooks inside your body, and you resent the lack of light in you. Little stones of transmission. Slow Poetry in America comes forward. Steps in time with optimism formed long ago. Look through lens-like prisms for distorted images of the long travail of an accidental purchase of skill. It's useless to intervene on the dream-work. There are moods in many crooked walks. Mission. Castro. Noe. Haight. Learn the art of invisibility. Navigate the sure heat of disintegration. Deny not your affirmations. And never silence your negations.

TEXAZONICO

There is a tense range of surrounding blankness. What ghosts of the past estrange us?

Hoa (pronounced *Wa*) and I left San Francisco to start a new life together. We put our things into a van. Traversed the Mojave. Arizona. New Mexico. Texas. Rugged escarpment intruded on words and the no words that shape a coming tense.

A late afternoon cloudbank throws shadows on the desert.

A quiet passage. Sotol. Kestrel. Sky.

The forlorn heat and signs of Interstate travel
persist by quick glimpse: flyby adobe red
pale yellow Terlingua twining pathways.
An hour or more for Holiday Inn lounge.
A place to sit. Cold drinks. Tortilla soup.
Across pink-orange plains *para* Texazonico.

Enter the unnamable name of the poem. The active tense of to be. And then onward crafting illusion out of syntax, performances shaped out of place. Craft a mirage like a history or signatures between signaling relations of inside and out. Name specific crafts of careful illusion. Make way for now comes Slow Poetry in America.

IN A DELIVERY VAN

I kept a yellow notepad and pencils, and when traffic slowed I wrote poems about Cabeza de Vaca and his traumatic entry into the Americas. My hand on the wheel, I listened to the streets and traffic, writing.

I reached out through Slow Poetry in America to know and see what rested underground—under soil, rock, oak. A naked baptism and conversion. Four Europeans in the flat coastal plains of South Texas. The loss of five hundred men, raving into the Gulf Stream, salty brine in their mouths. And sunlight. Bleak sunlight on barren coast. Sand. Heat and cold. Their knowledge and labor, virtues and faith, conceived in the tiny dramas and initiations of desire and skill. All absorbed into the sea and then nothing of it left to see.

At one moment, the four survivors remove their armor and weapons, strip naked, load makeshift rafts and push out into November water. The cold surf chafes them; the wind and foam and suds dog their efforts. Rafts tip, sink. The men return to the beach, wet and exposed. They have nothing and are newly deposited into a past their histories have not transacted. Man on rock, sand, wooden pieces, shells.

The aboriginals took pity when they met the Europeans. They wept with them in the cold air and sat close together, embracing the naked wetness of the strangers.

Fires were lit strategically, and the Europeans were guided to each in a line toward a village encampment. Smoke in the air, in the hair and skin of these people. Structures of grass and hides withheld fire and skins and smoke and grease. A womb of smoky darkness and dim light of fires flashing against an alien blur of attention distributed among them.

Nothing here. No thing but things and the gestures of endurance turned object. To see. To be given sight. Again. Into natural objects. Not 'natural' not 'nature.' A nature alien like some animal come to life to cleave at the soul. The no soul of European design. The great architecture corroded. A cathedral of the mind come undone. Stringy meat. Insects mashed into a paste. A man not man. To see hands, arms, feet. Not other. A portion of landscape. A sickness, disease, shared, relieved in the incantations of a voice. No voice. Voices shared. No other.

Not speech. A voice in the voices. Composing the muddy substance of one being. A non-being. The endurance of the senses organized by a larger form they compose. Air and sand; rock and wind. The psychic shield of the body's ability to gather, barter, trade. In the wilderness of eternity where Time died in them. Every day a fire. Muscle. A submerged imaginary come alive.

Writing these mysteries threatened the movements of the van over highway and urban streets. Slow Poetry in America said to me, Focus on the road. I carried a bouquet into a law office on Congress Avenue. The receptionist thanked me, offering a butterscotch candy.

BLACK WALNUTS

There was a bungalow on Higgins Street in Austin
we moved into and our children were born there.
Hoa painted covers and I stamped the name *Skanky*
Possum on the little zines we mailed. Eleven years
in an East Side cul-de-sac, living next door to Fuzzy
and Bubba, and across the street from Chop-Chop
and Fairy and Fey who eyed the boys as they played
in hackberry shade, and under the slender limbs of
desert willow.

The many years accumulate and decay with swift urgency. A time
to take leave came almost by surprise. The books went into storage.
A June fire toasted hotdogs and s'mores, the boys dripping wet
from the hose and a blue, plastic pool cooled them in the shade.
Low the pecan limbs hanged, and black walnuts. Kissed
the barky trunks of them all goodbye. Said words like, So long,

my friends, and pressed palms flat against rough
  skin. And the leaves
played light on my face. Goodbye, Dear Ones,
  we said.

ALBATROSS

In Chris Jordan's photographs baby albatross bellies are filled with plastic trash. Cameras document their distorted figures—making signatures of a moment in duress. How might we 'process' such figurative associations of cheap industrial detritus bound within the organic tissue of expired creatures? They feed on bright doodads and shards, colorful pieces of discarded parts: clear syringe; worn balloon fragments; shampoo and detergent bottle tops; blue packing straw; medicine dropper; green, red, and yellow, translucent Bic lighters; aqua-colored Styrofoam pieces; buttons; a little bear; soda tops; engine oil container lids. A detached sacrum rises out of decayed feathers and the patterns of modernity accumulate in the rot on black pebbles, a thin albatross bill extending eyeless gaze toward the photographer's foot. These entrails make weird auguries: the refuse of industrial and post-industrial forms spiral outward toward a still too-slow-to-learn wilderness of exposed beings. Witness the accumulated residues of life-as-usual, unconscious, earnest in its need; examine the foreclosed judgments determined by arrangements of parti-colored fragments that choke the host. The optimistic urge to embrace modernity collapses in the far, unseen reaches of a world unused to such forward-looking endeavors. The decayed feathers and rotted portions of flesh reveal nothing but a mortality belonging to us, too.

Friends arrive. We drink wine. I wonder about us in a merriment that skims the surface of some deeper experience. The faces in the scrapbooks of my family—what will they hope to find to redeem the albatross exhaustion? The moments when we learn that our habits produce suffering pass rapidly. And yet, it's like discovering nuclear bombs: the knowledge integrates into associations we make with the world. Our experience bloats with the random accumulations of particles we are fed. Icebergs melt; islands shrink; tsunamis suck bodies into the deep. We know this. And move on. And store the knowledge. And forget. And are reminded. And upon our deaths, when our torsos are exposed, the auguries of this knowledge present what we knew, and what the birds told us, on the pebbles, decaying with their firm particles next to the lumbar bones and skull fragments. No one in the 1930s would have considered this, not until Catastrophe hit. Hopefulness made a strict ideology of discipline, attention, and mindless drive to move outward in a world where there was an out. What do the albatross think? Their ancient patterns continue without thought to the accumulating plastic in their bellies. In Jordan's photos there are maps of a future and a present. I hear Donny Green's voice and his taunting about dick hair. I hear my grandfather's worried voice as I view the pictures of bodies in India. I look and I watch with great wonder. We are so small next to things erupting around us. I stare into these dead things, and dream of the life still there.

GREEK TOWN

Everything had been left in disarray: boxes, furniture, sacks and bags of our casual and intimate belongings. The refrigerator hummed sadly, quite empty, except for some bottles of sports drink, yellowish green, one nearly all drunk up by the movers who, the day before, grunted and cussed, fussing their way up stairs with bookshelves and bedposts. The driver chain-smoked, directing the young blacks he'd picked up in Scarborough around corners and to watch the fuck out not to scratch anything. His son died in a boating accident, he told me, smoking on the front stoop. The Irish neighbors on one side, the Greeks on the other: they watched as our things were unpacked in the front yard and carried in, the large semi parked in part on the curb. A humid air seeped with grey clouds from over the south, out of the expanse of Lake Ontario.

At one point during the long expulsion of clutter and crap hauled out of the States I walked down the street (one kilometer it says here on Google Maps) to a pub and ordered my first drink in Greek Town. I was sweaty, clammy. The place hummed, or maybe buzzed, pretty well for a Thursday afternoon. I was too tired to study it or its inhabitants. The spirit I ordered was carefully measured in a little shot glass.

A theme of sweat accumulates the first month or so, the final weeks of the Ontario summer. Slowly, the little pieces fall in place, the bigger ones doing as they usually do, spreading out, elaborating, jarring into the background of every day, until habits resume, routines stabilize into concrete, forgetful rituals. I had been looking for an art of the invisible, a perfectly sutured or transparent possibility of resistance: an art beside life turned inside out, so that art no longer mattered because it, like life, exists only in fragments, gestures, quick glimpses. So I set myself a task: to inspect inward drives and compelling curiosities; in other words, I attended the things that wouldn't allow me to shut up. Besides that, my life had fallen to pieces; fragments that matter only to me and some friends, my family. More importantly, I found myself situated further north on the continent: here people spoke differently, moved their bodies under the shade of large maples and elms, yes, quite different indeed from the brushy scrub of South Texas. Their legs reached out over the concrete like lengthy Nordic poems, only the ethnic backgrounds were Southeast Asian, Eastern European, Caribbean, African. The complexity of character jolted the quiet rituals of the daily goings-on. Even the squirrels came in new colors, grey and black, both tremendously fat, swollen on garden veggies and the fruits of the backyards of Toronto.

In the mornings, I rode off on my bike down Danforth and Bloor to Sherbourne, and went south to Gerrard, which took me all the way to Victoria St. An art, like an elixir, or alchemic substance, distills, or, more often, disrupts, from its non-existent state inside the dull cranium. Perhaps it lies dormant in the regulatory depths of the fatty brain. Breathe deeply; absorb the radiant (though damp) heat of the city.

I have landed from Outer Space to study the people of North America, said the Man at Yonge and Dundas, holding a sign. But the sign didn't make the signal. The circuitry outside Sears and the Hard Rock Café generated a symbolic kinesis that, like a web, spread over everything there. No one seemed to notice, but I listened. In those early weeks, I found a pattern like the movement of the sun, or the slow transit of Venus over the face of the sun. A gravitational pull of sorts oriented the various public and private actions taking place. A bus roared by; taxis stopped abruptly in the bike lane; the homeless and hustlers on Jarvis quite early in the morning offered business curbside; and potholes made biking difficult. Slow Poetry in America continued.

A LIGHT ON THE WALL

A breeze moves through curtains making a flickering lace of light on the wall. Observe its narrow shapes, elongated, thin. A cinematic flame in the evening display of forms. I watch the light while Hoa sleeps, her body resting under sheets. Lift my fingers to my eyes, covering them. And then open. Thin flame of light kinetic and glowing in flowing waves of movement. The inside and outside merge then separate. My hands, legs; her neck, arms, and the dark hair on her forehead. Between us and the wall a light moves and the breeze through curtains contains my attention in the room in summer in Ontario. Maples through the window. Silver Maples. Sometimes you see what you think you see and then other times you see what the object outside you demands you see. In the merger of the quiet of the meeting of yourself with the other. The narrow flame shifts and the light dims with dusk. Awakening and Aversion. The movement as if a sound visualized at the edge of consciousness. As she sleeps and I get up from the sheets to leave the room.

LOON

Dusk. No breeze. Maples and white pine and birches' silver skin shine from the dense green.

Three loons coast twenty feet from the canoe.

At night, Slow Poetry in America the Loon calls forlornly across the darkness of the lake. During the morning, while swimming with my sons, the loons call out from the woods. By afternoon, one lands near us, gliding to a stop. It floats out, black head and white breast, bobbing on the wake left by boats. Long glissandos rise over the water as the loon moves out on the glassy surface, lowers its head: it vanishes under water. A moment later it re-emerges forty yards to the south of us.

The loons' calls of distress reach out of the late night darkness. The sounds follow the coastline and spread above the surface of the water and the invisible distances I imagine from the dock. Ghost Loon of America, of the Canadian Shield withholding its water in igneous chains that lock us tight to the continent. Invisible presence of the Old Loon of America, Grandaddy Loon of the granite imaginary.

Again a loon calls across the water. Again come the soundings of indifferent origins astounding the woodsy pace of North Ontario.

A LITTLE STORM

A sudden shower: hail. Boys play in a tent as the rain intensifies. The lake blurs in silver and grey sheets of water.

The boys delight in the wild of the air. A moment of escape from the every day into the Slow Poetry in America of the wood and lake and loons. Wind sends pulsations through the tent. A Mesmer of attention. Light in the maple canopy.

Along the granite lip of the Ontario North thunder travels over the hills and through the trees. A creature breathes with raspy endurance. Air and water and mud cohering into a pattern of physical being.

Exposed to the elements of the North. My children perceive the animated air, the gravity of earth. The giant needle of the compass leads vision to the upper climates. Canada's expansive figurations of wilderness are held in the currents of cold in the air and lake of the being of the North. Slow Poetry in America moves out in the wind and thunder. The poets of place are sensitive to careful movements and patient labors. The boys also coil into a piney fragrance of being and not being sure of anything they see. The poets write or they do not write; speak or no speech is uttered. To create from the mists and furzy undergrowth, ferns dripping in the ivy-covered loams, a thin topsoil composed from beneath by a granite thickness more ancient than the icy mass that opened the lakes and hills and eyes of the northern shield.

There is another kind of storm, one of metaphoric, and also very real, complexity. Catastrophe has many forms, and it's difficult to avoid implication in any of them. To the American imagination, Canada is a land of liberal decency, though the term 'liberal' has lost significant power as guiding proposition: to be liberal is to be at self-righteous ease as calamitous events multiply under the heavy boot of corporate empire. I can react in horror to the farmer in India who swallows insecticide, but I do nothing to contest those companies who pressure Asian markets with genetically modified seed. I can eat from my organic garden, but the suicides multiply, and debts to western corporations and governments grow. It is possible to isolate feeling from the magnitude of events that snare thought in terrible traps. Better to hide behind liberal platitudes than to violate belief with the dystopia of self-scrutiny. But such scrutiny is necessary, for no border defines national determination. Something as facile as the phrase 'national character' easily covers up the more sinister implications of what it means to live comfortably in the West. It is far better to perform a radical overturning of how we understand our motives in the larger geopolitical relationships that sustain the circulations of products, both material and ideological—an extreme shock or violence of determination, by which to see. The threat of affliction, whether by nuclear bomb or religious terror, is used to fabricate an inward fear, one that justifies the liberal surface exposure to evil. The daily abstraction of mediated events distorts those more isolated emergencies, for violence is real in its intimacy, not as a conceptual exertion of force. The drones hovering over Yemen promise an end to terror even as, for too many, a terror of mutilation weaves into the fabric of social existence, engendering further violence, in circuits of a future unwinding with tremendous speed.

Another way to put it might be: how do I cultivate dignity even in direct view of violence—though perhaps this also is an undignified wish? The hard task of dismantling one's projections, of taking apart the abstract values that pass as one's own, requires vigilant thought, like Whalen's constant observation of the process of perception—a self contained by its own limited conditions. An affirmation and aversion, a dependency on the new.

I see my children move on hard granite toward the little lake. They swim at great cost, and with terrific luxury, in a humble region of isolated forest. I used to think I could leave the United States to begin a new life without its tentacles reaching through me. I thought Mexico or the Middle East promised a better possibility. But there's no escaping what is absorbed in all the years that compose the reactive nature of a person. To see the world through the eyes of others, to see oneself in the stance of other people, at other moments in the deterioration of an interior memory where time is composed, here in such a poetry, no reconciliation exists: each day is addressed wholly new, on its terms, in a tense oscillation between mood and experience, the terminal interstices of self-reliance.

The long anxious days of wanting to know what lay just out of reach suddenly transforms. You feel as though you've grasped some new thing, a kind of knowledge or ability to transform, move out into another possibility. Writing is a task and a constant threat. You arrive, and then you leave. And you are alone, submerged in a self that is not there when the writing is real. An internal turning, and inside-outing. Clear as goldenrod growing. As white pine and maple, beech and birch. The forest of varied apprehensions: forget-me-nots and lilac. 'Nothing lasts,' clichés, 'truth' 'as if'.... 'The images set off down the road and yet they never get anywhere.' Until they do, and you do, momentarily. It is a problem of time and perception, of witness and release—a reshaping into action. Soft pine needles spongy under your feet. The deposits and decay and heat in the soil. Modernities and publics—great cancerous attacks against images. To contain, control, discipline. What 'I' am hardly matters in the writing. A 'writing' or 'reading' is a defense against a sense of time measured by the growth of trees and the soil stirred into being by the fallen leaves and needles of many ages. Energy and heat. A day at a lake. My wife reading in another room. A room in a future where children will play. A room in a past life where I was a child playing with the manufactures of my culture: war heroes, action figures—the imaginaries of power and hierarchy. Learning a discipline to turn thought back on the mind. Dislodge. A wind on the lake in the leaves of the birch and maple and white pine. Dirt and mulch and brush.

MIGRANTS

Wake to the chatter of children. We adhere to shift-
ing narratives that hold momentarily.
  A violent lake monster from Oxtongue breathes
  Fire between pines. Watercolor dries.
  Look between lines. Go behind words.
  As witnesses to events migrate through time
  let the record show: dispersed leaves; a lit
  November sidewalk (freshly cemented);
  black squirrels clinging to bare pear limbs;
  and voices of children like the chorus of myself
  remixed and replayed in dissolute loops.
  A mistook clarity. Light the illusive fest....

WILDERNESS

At Dundas and Yonge the movement of people intensifies as daylight increases. Sometimes I wander here, or sit on a bench across from Eaton Centre. I live so far north on the continent now, on the edge of Lake Ontario. A woman brings her children into a Canadian Tire. Jamaicans and Persians and other races migrate daily routines into the climates of the north. Toronto is a blended place. Its identity adheres with Slow Poetry in America. It is a wilderness of refugees, stunned by the force of the modern. The Tunisian merchants on the Danforth convey the indifference of North America. Men in thick beards attend Mosque near the LCBO during Ramadan. Serb churches and Estonian community centers stand out among the Anglican lines of the city streets and the neighborhoods of detached and semi-detached homes, narrowly packed into city allotments. As a nation, Canada's commitments to Capital are in line with violent policies to the south. But as an imaginary of the north, Ontario folds into a wilderness past, willing a wild survival in the refugees and immigrants that come to Toronto from other disabled and destroyed *zonas* of human misery.

In the afternoon, I bike to the ferry terminal and then go to Wards Island. I arrive at a beach where children play in the water and from the shore you see the wide stretch of the lake and nothing on the other side is visible. The America of my mind is desolate. America is here, too, a living presence. With the African, Asian, and European clash. Who I am and what I'm not. The Slow Poetry of self-realization intertwined with the subtle geographies and cultural histories aligned or misaligned in the vagaries of climate and want. There is a drive to appear and to vanish; the will and the want to oversee some physical presence; a genuine awakening of the body to the body, bringing thought to reclaim provisory divisions. The soul interferes with wilderness. Icy water spreads on my feet and my ankles. People splash in the cold surf, and children build sand castles with beach pebbles, moss, and sticks. A boy eats a smoothie in the shade; egrets land in distance birch tops. Arranged and complicit in the many errors of belief, no one can just drop out. Art by itself cannot account for its internal, mimetic terms: the conditions in which it comes into being distort individual effort. Slow Poetry in America requires social action—an applied presssure. It cannot be copied or manufactured; no style defines its patterns. It is embedded with potential, and risks failure or incoherence to achieve something momentarily defined.

SLOW POETRY IN AMERICA THE COOT

Slow Poetry in America the coot. Slow Poetry in America the live oak. Slow Poetry in America the chipmunk. Slow Poetry in America the crow. Slow Poetry in America Niagara. Slow Poetry in America Duck Creek. Slow Poetry in America Brazos River. Slow Poetry in America Colorado. Slow Poetry in America white pine. Slow Poetry in America balsam. Slow Poetry in America birch. Slow Poetry in America Lake Huron and Lake Simcoe. Slow Poetry in America the moon. The moon. Yes, the moon. The feminine necessity of America.

SOME RUDIMENTARY NOTES

North American society absorbs acute distress at an increasingly rapid pace even as global culture seems barely poised for the violent pitches heaved by some apparently drunk, or maimed, perhaps an exceedingly deranged, pitcher (the metaphor's a stretch, I know). It's difficult to know how to direct energy, to enable counteractive magics, to encourage outrageous action, to inspire rational reflection, to generate intelligent deliberation, to manage careful attention, all wagered in a delirium of violence, shock, fear, and loss that increasingly define contemporary horizons.

The recycled gestures of the avant-garde veer toward exhaustion in contemporary contexts. Poetry's archaic possibilities might re-emerge with new pressure instead. The availability of new gestures through art provides ways of organizing a line, a sentence, an utterance, an argument. Language recedes behind the value of words. Words perform services to the emergent energies and emotions that associate the adhering forms of experience and imagination, invention and happenstance.

Poetry identifies what must not be spoken, and brings those words out regardless with right timing. *Kairos*, the sudden and timely delivery of the right utterance or gesture, relieves us for a moment, re-orients how we feel or think. In a cultural moment where lies are spread in plain sight, where privilege and power gain advantage on truth and justice, poets may have the skills of inquiry to intervene, at least for a moment, to keep new bodies of feeling alive where we barter modes of care for fleeting, even delusional, claims of relevance. We must outpace institutional claims, and yet often we crawl through the bureaucratic passages, as Melville said, like flies in a skull.

KOSHLONG

Alone on the road under pines and maples deer flies bite; mosquitoes pester us. My son is tired, gives out. Dennis leads us to a slice of granite, where we sit. After a moment he says, 'Let's build an inukshuk to let the others know we've passed by.'

We gather flat stones and rounder ones. At base two flat pieces of granite make the feet. Stack other rocks and flakes of rock until the form of a person coheres.

The little stone figure peeks out of the goldenrod surrounding him. Patiently she waits, the sound of wind and flies and summer light filtering over a stony body.

Later, when the others finally meet us at the cottage, we ask if they had seen the inukshuk we left for them. No, they say, they had not, having taken, instead, another path to the beaver dams and through the brush that had marked their legs with red abrasions.

We jumped off the dock into Lake Koshlong. A ring of granite. The children splashed. Hoa took a boogie board and swam out in the direction of Turtle Rock.

STONES

I've been looking to the past for an invention, or
relation. A new world as metaphor of return: failure
is not an option—failure is required.
   Garden or wilderness, the ancient and archaic
   ruins. Lay a stone foundation by
   lilac and by aster. Tiny figure squats
   among granite chips. As if to come or go
   home. So to point direction and follow
   or to hasten the waste. Comes the heat of day
   now, solid. White pine, balsam, deer fly.

CANADIAN SHIELD

Jet skis slice across the lake and crank cascades of motor reverb across the loony water. The house next to us is ginormous: three floors, decks, panel siding, elegant eaves, and storm windows. A little dock hosts water toys and boats and the glassy surface of the lake is intruded on by a radio of urban bandwidth until late at night.

Morgan and I drink under a pine by the water and listen to the radio cutting the air between us. The expense of division, construction, and commute distorts the attraction of the granite and green. We are fleshy in our dream of the quiet. But barbed wire is strung around any quiet place that is quiet too long (a problem of what sells and what will not). My thoughts adhere to the image of the garden, but the garden is fenced and secured with apparatuses of intent. And a wilderness grows up inside of things. At first little ivy sprouts burst fragile stems, and soon they are hairy arms thickening into the greenery and decay of abandoned beliefs. And in the woods are spirits, half thought, or abandoned, come

to reclaim their sovereignty against your corny need.
Slow Poetry in America, the refuse of broken things.

Slow Poetry in America echoed through the swing set pipes. My son put his ear to the metal and listened to the creaking of the hinges that reverberated in the frame structure. We played at the sea monster park on 45th St in Austin. Both children chased me to the slide, the tube slide—the blue one. When they exited I would reach out and growl. Squeals of delight followed them away as they escaped my sea monster fists.

Often we bought doughnuts at Mrs Johnson's on Airport Blvd. The city spread out its expanses of green and concrete between cell phone towers. The Sri Lankan behind the counter seemed exhausted; a face on him that suggested he must have been up all night as he stamped out little bits of dough and sugar. Sweat or grease pressed down his shiny hair. He rarely brightened as we entered, but he gave us extra doughnuts or doughnut holes. I preferred maple; Keaton chocolate cream filled; Waylon chocolate glazed. Knowing this makes a difference. It slows down the world. These are not precise descriptions. Descriptions are rarely precise. Writing makes suggestions, hints at what is probable, to shape or define a situation with illusions. One day, perhaps, if I should read these words again, I'll see the doughnut flavors and remember eating our breakfast on Fridays in the park on 45th with a sudden pressure of affection for what will be lost to me then.

We ate our doughnuts on a bench under an oak before I turned into a monster. Broken light drifted through the branches. Often other children joined our games. In summer we'd sometimes break from the playground and jump into the municipal pool. We'd leave smelling of chlorine and sunscreen and metal.

It's odd to look back at those moments from a short distance. Or to see back further to myself on the backyard swing set where I played and listened for Slow Poetry in America of the mulberry leaves. Only I didn't know Slow Poetry in America was alive in the sounds and scents and visions then.

My children run to the far side of the park. Their bare feet slap the short, brittle grass. They tag a pecan tree and return, laughing, pulling on each other to slow the other down.

In the time that is no time to memory or imagination I often revisit the park. Waylon, last week in northern Ontario, on a hike, sat down on the dirt path trembling, weeping, as only an eight-year-old can. I miss the sea monster park, he said, and held me under the shades of white pine and maple, in that alien northern forest.

O, my love, what have we to compare ourselves to? A quick drifting through each other's lives? O, my love, we are here among America's things.

ALIEN DRIFT

A crisp, bright day. Children play and mothers accompany the younger ones under bare oak limbs. Shadows everywhere. I look or imagine looking through their eyes or their children's eyes toward the blunt metal surfaces of playground equipment. Above us a hawk's white belly broadens, its wings wide, pale underneath. A few speckled red-brown feathers spot its breast: the same rust color darkens along the upper body as it turns, gliding in the warmer currents of air that make it buoyant without, it seems, any effort at all.

I try to look at me through the eyes of these mothers. I try to look back in time through my mother's eyes to me as I was to her. I wander through her eyes and wonder what I am to her now, and look again. The bright day warms. And children play tag and spin.

Sometimes there is something alien that drifts through the years. It is apprehended only by others and evades any personal effort to gain some glimpse of its form. I like to think I have changed and yet the part of me that does mutate is accompanied by something that will not. What 'I' am hardly matters, though 'it' does seem to possess a playfulness, a kind of charmed echo, of all the things forgotten and lost in the dimness of memory.

A new hawk joins the other. Both pale breasts and bottom wings spread nearby. I bring my son close: we look at the birds together as their arcs widen. Maybe they're looking for lunch, I say. Yes, he says, maybe. What will they find, I say. A mouse maybe, says my son. A mouse indeed, I say. Aren't you hungry? Shouldn't we get lunch? Yes, he says, but not a mouse. No, I say, no mouse lunch for me.

Across the playground, my other son calls for me to push him in a swing. A girl spins in a large yellow cup. The mothers are leaving for lunch, though some have gathered with their children to eat on a picnic table. A Christmas wreath and ribbon stand out on a distant building. A boy tells his mother he will not leave and she threatens him. My son rides higher in the swing and the branches of the oaks cast shady streaks he breaks through.

Dale Smith has resided at various times in Texas, Yemen, Oregon, California, and Ontario. On the faculty of the Department of English at Ryerson University, Toronto, he has published essays, reviews, and criticism, including, most recently, *Poets Beyond the Barricade: Rhetoric, Citizenship, and Dissent after 1960*, and is the author of poetry texts that include *American Rambler, Black Stone,* and *Susquehanna*. His provocative arguments on the concept of Slow Poetry have been discussed in *The Atlantic, The Huffington Post,* and at other locations of literary and cultural debate.

Slow Poetry in America was designed and typeset in
Trump Mediäval by Kyle Schlesinger at Cuneiform Press.